Thank you for choosing our coloring book! We're thrilled to have you embark on a journey of creativity and relaxation. Each page was crafted with care to provide you with hours of artistic pleasure. Your support means the world to us, and we hope this book brings color to your days as much as your choice has brightened ours. Happy coloring!"

Lauro AC
2024

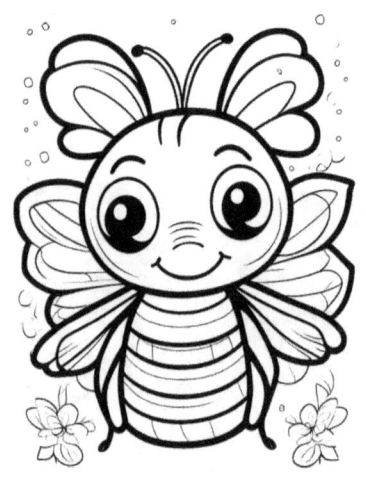
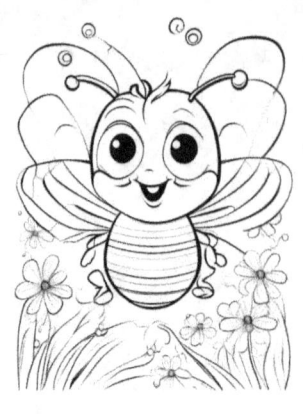

This Book Belongs to:

_____

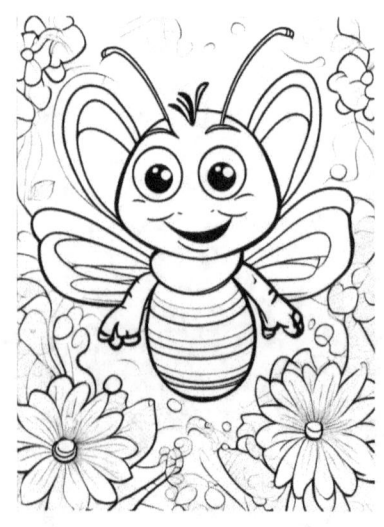
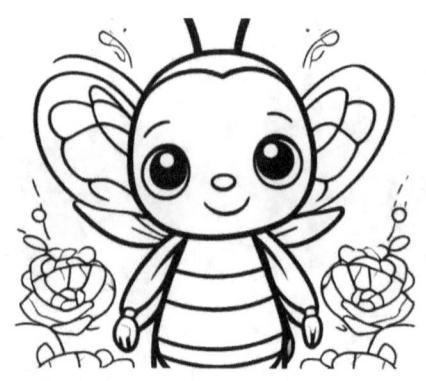

L.F.H.©
all rights reserved

ALL RIGHTS RESERVED©
2024

We want you to enjoy test! 📚✨ Please remember that the content of this book is protected by copyright. This means that it's not allowed to copy, share, or distribute any part of it without proper authorization. However, feel free to use small excerpts in your reviews or for educational purposes, as long as it's not for commercial gain. If you have any questions about what is permitted, it's always a good idea to get in touch with the publisher. Respecting copyright is about valuing creative work! 🖊️💁

©

L.F.H.
lauro'AC publications

Test Color Page

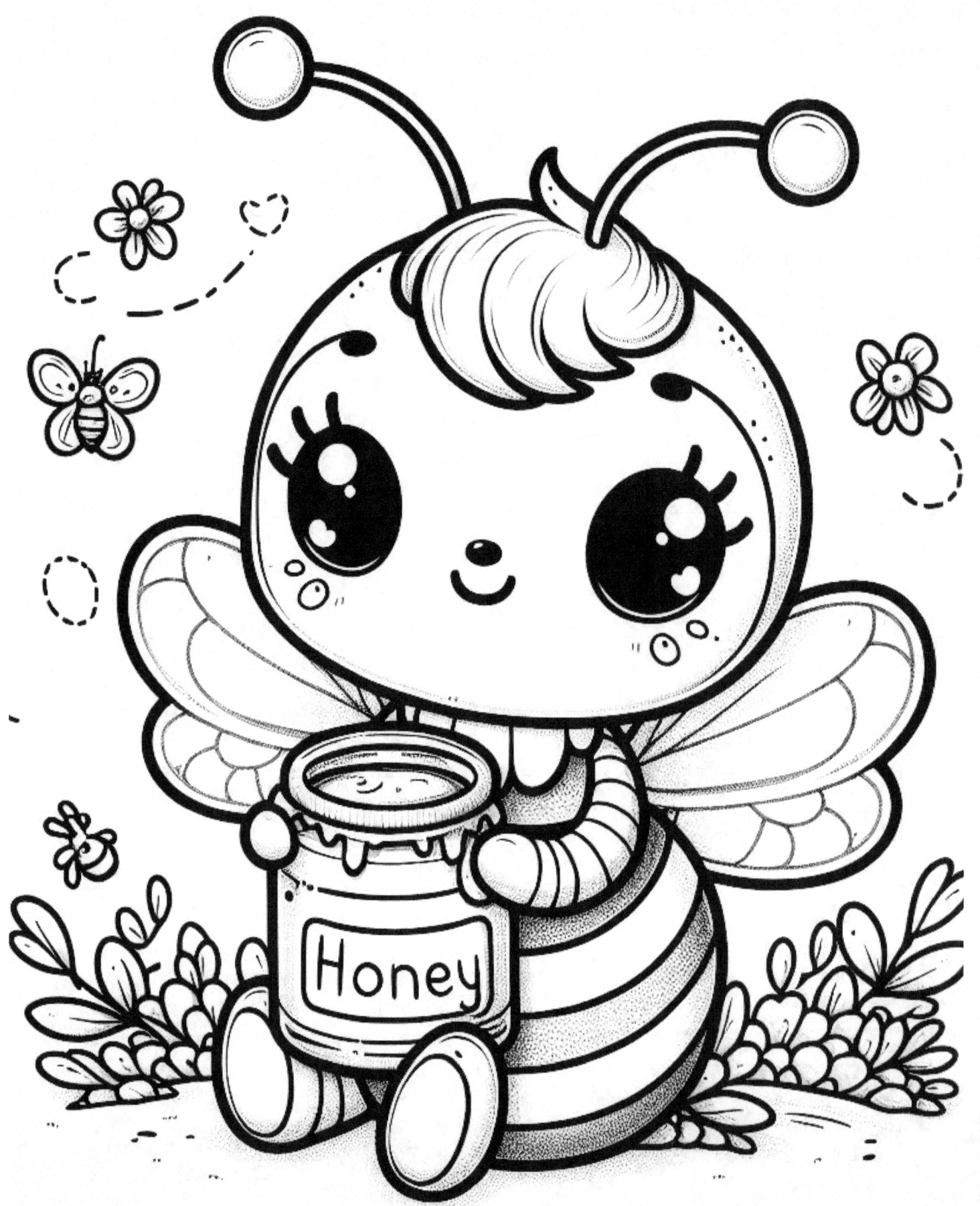

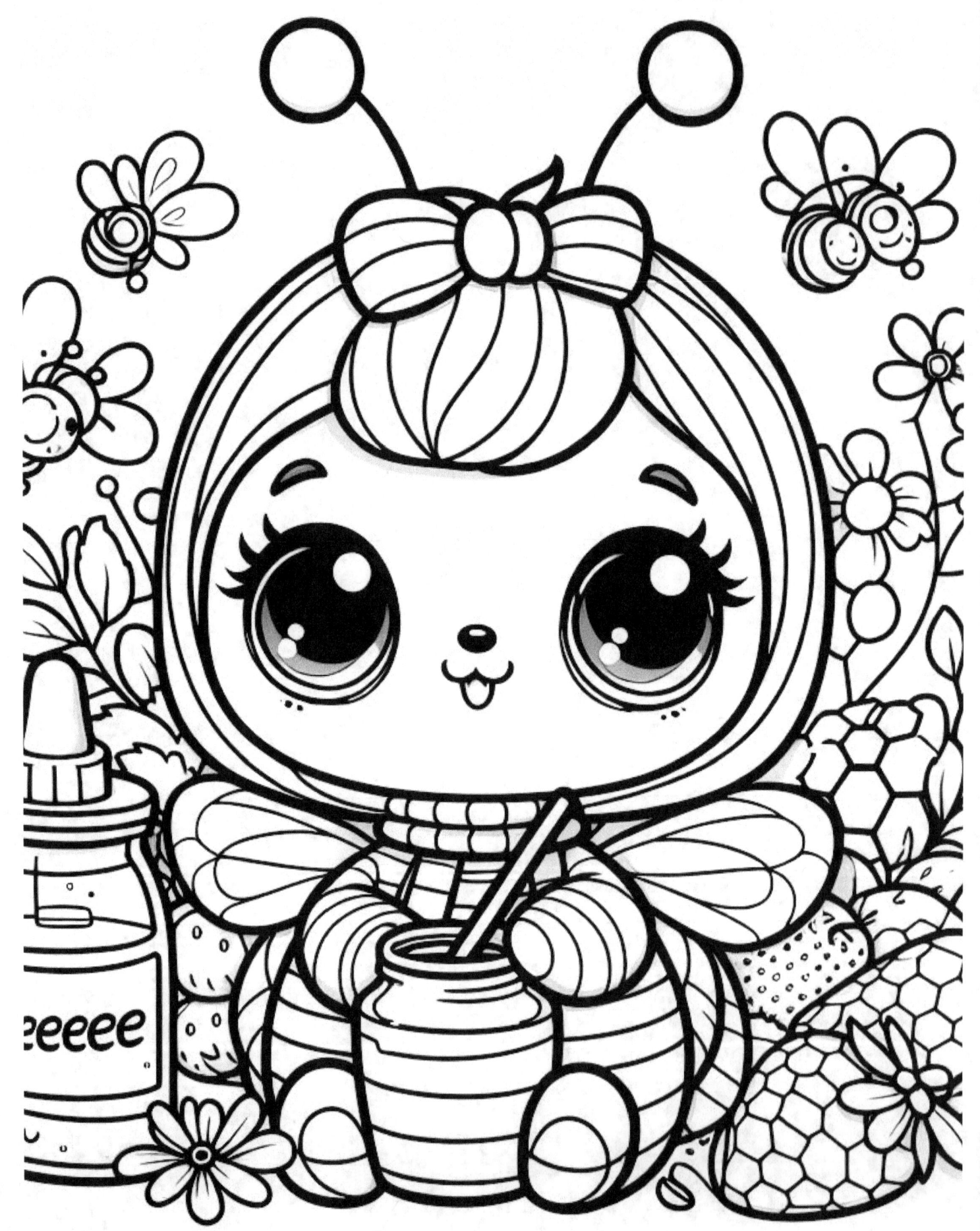

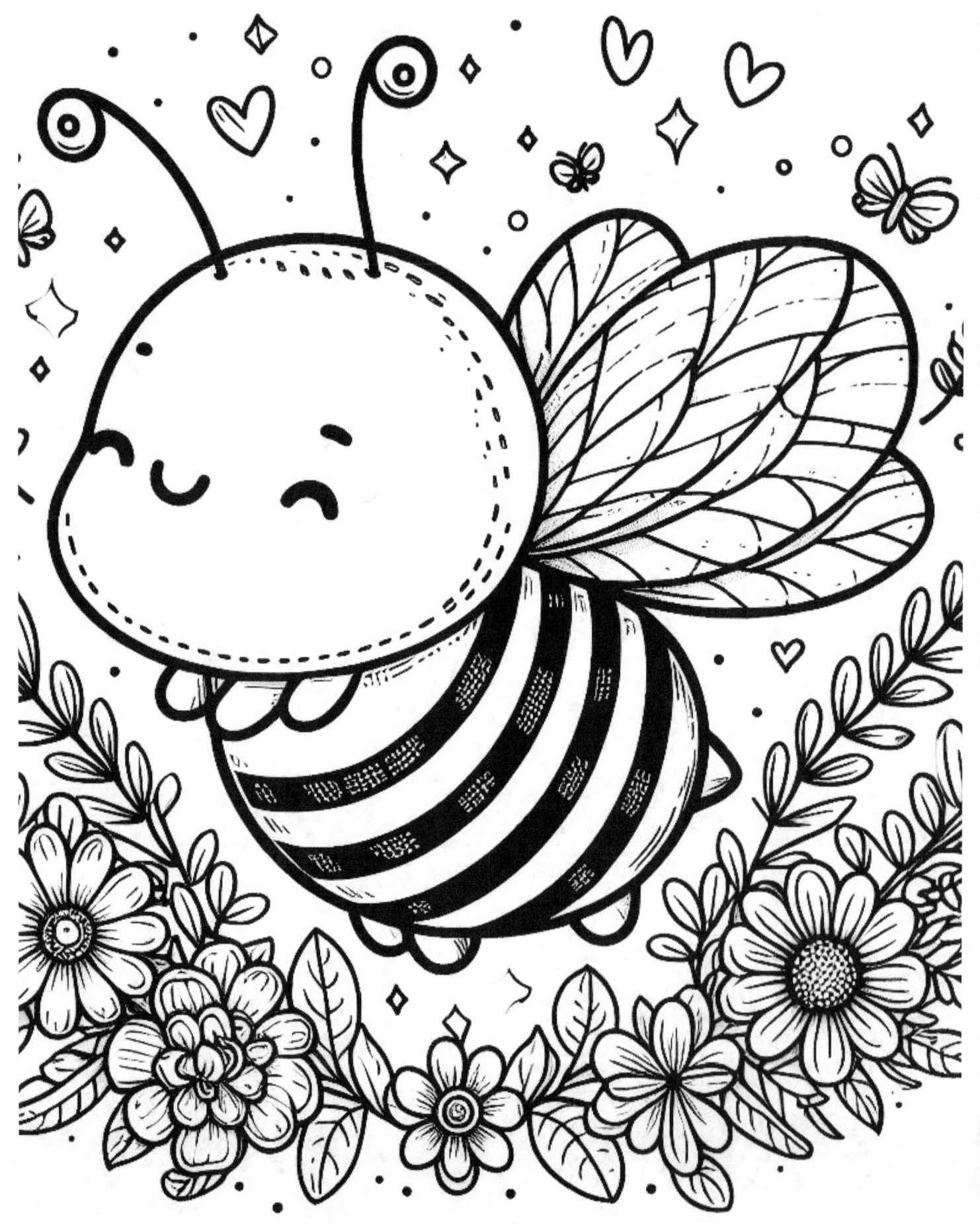

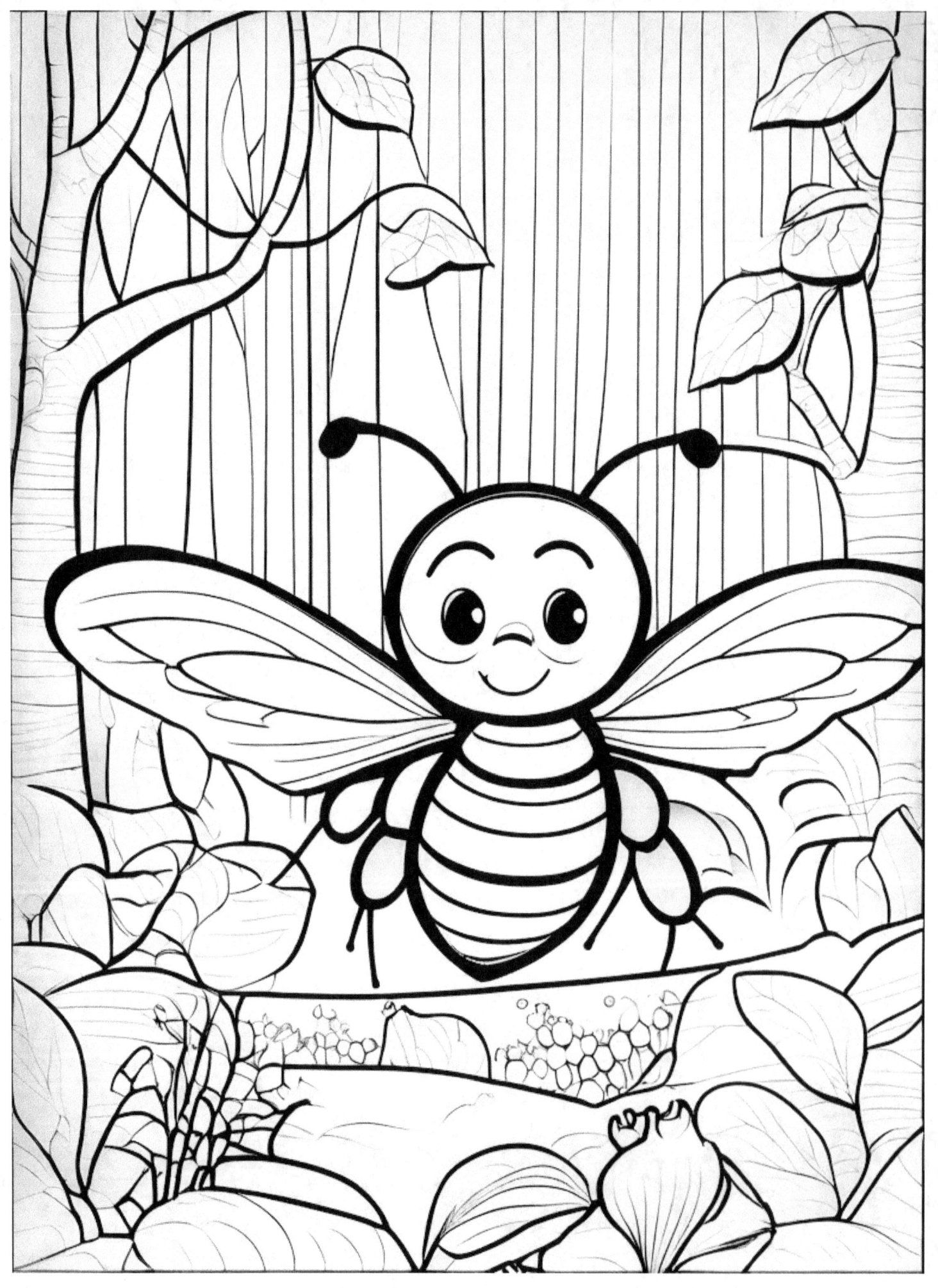

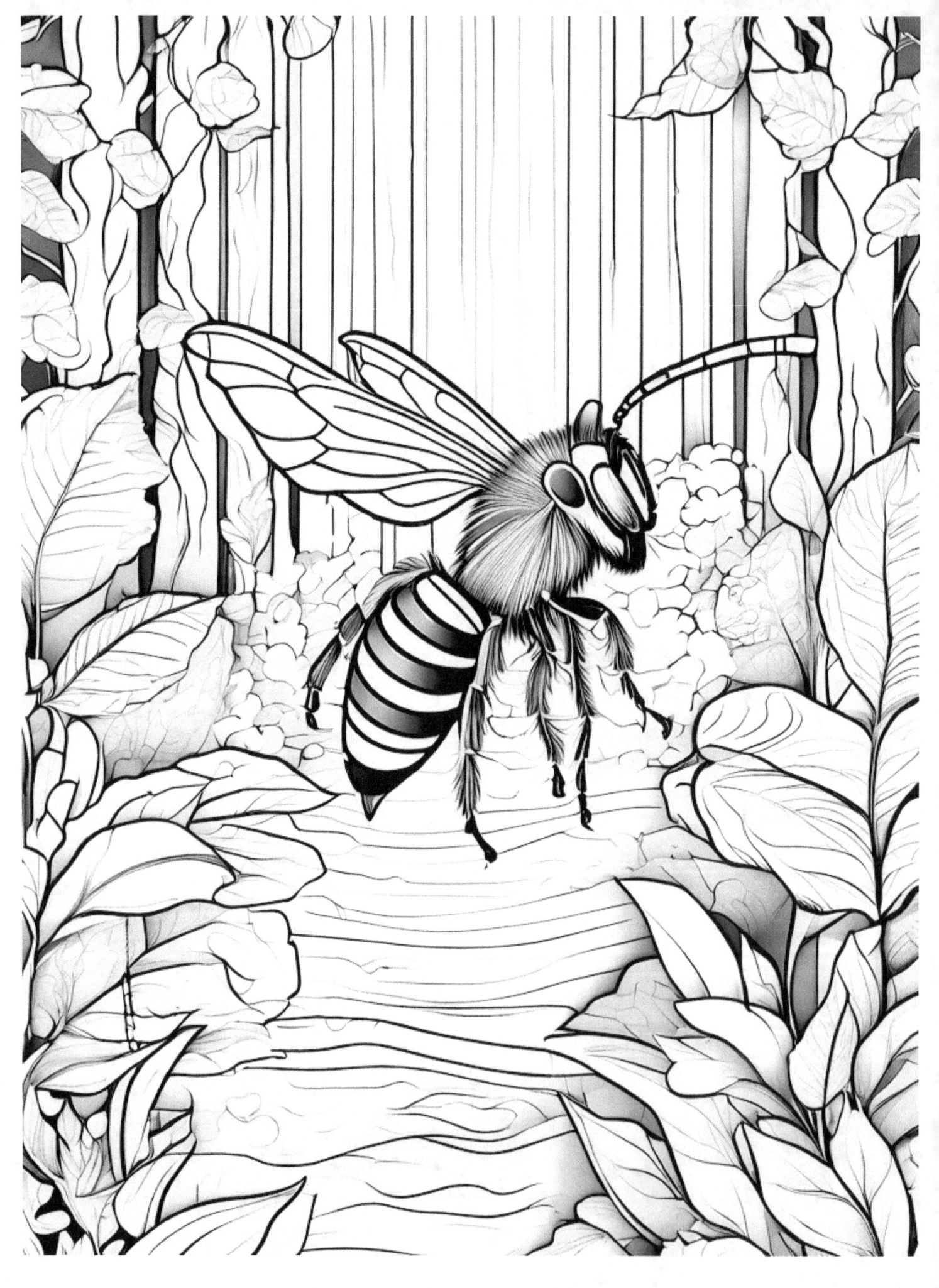

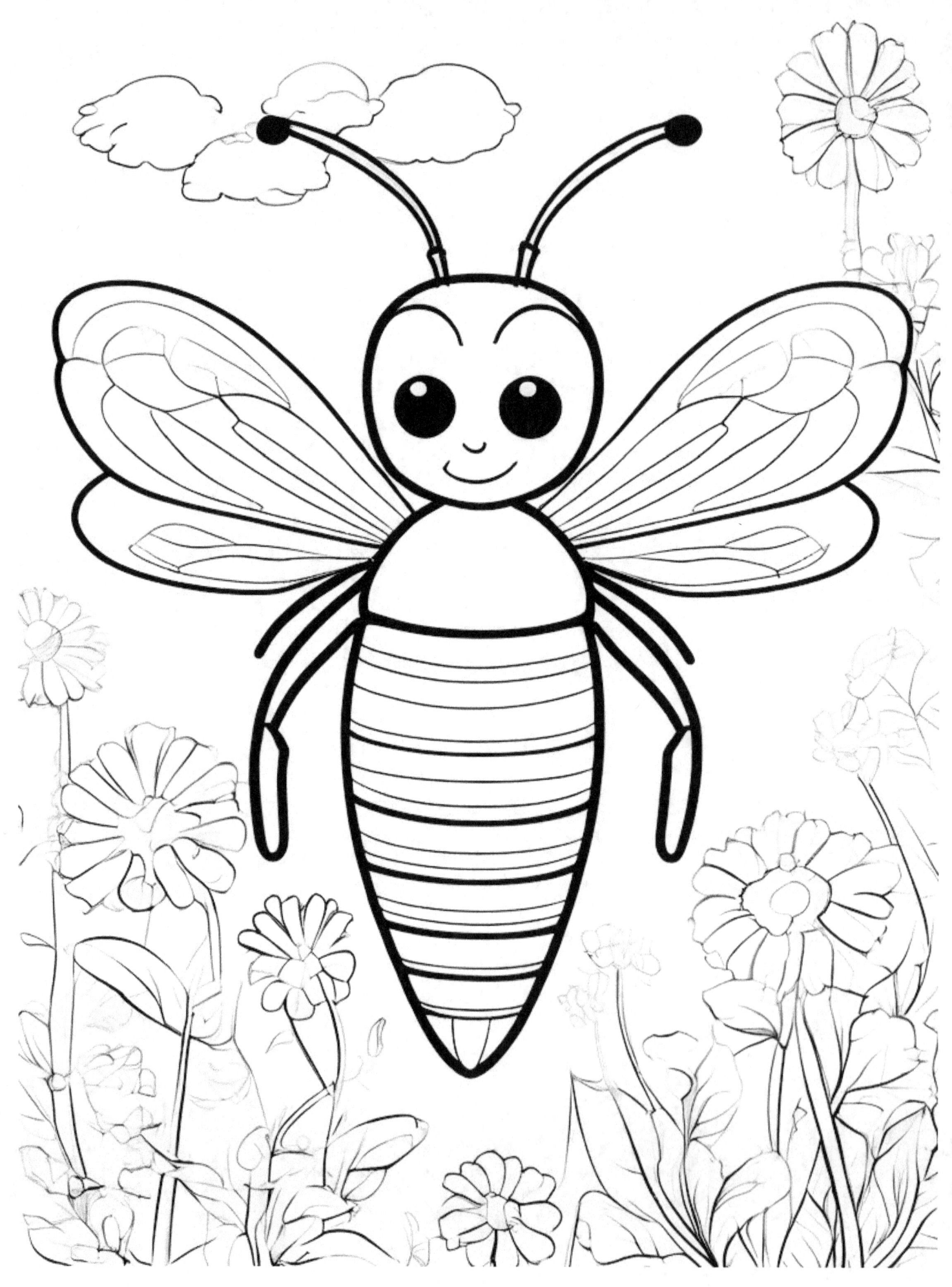

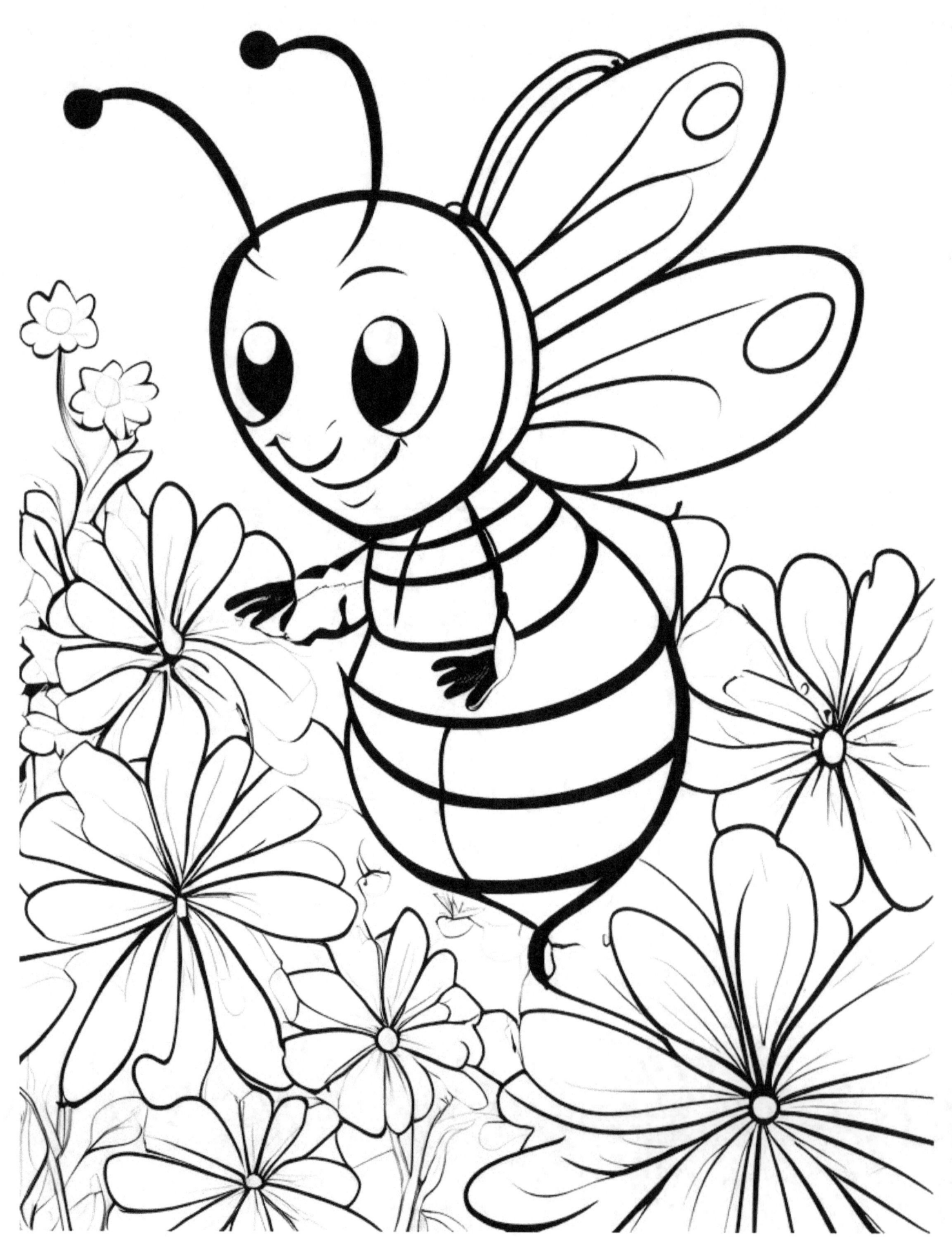

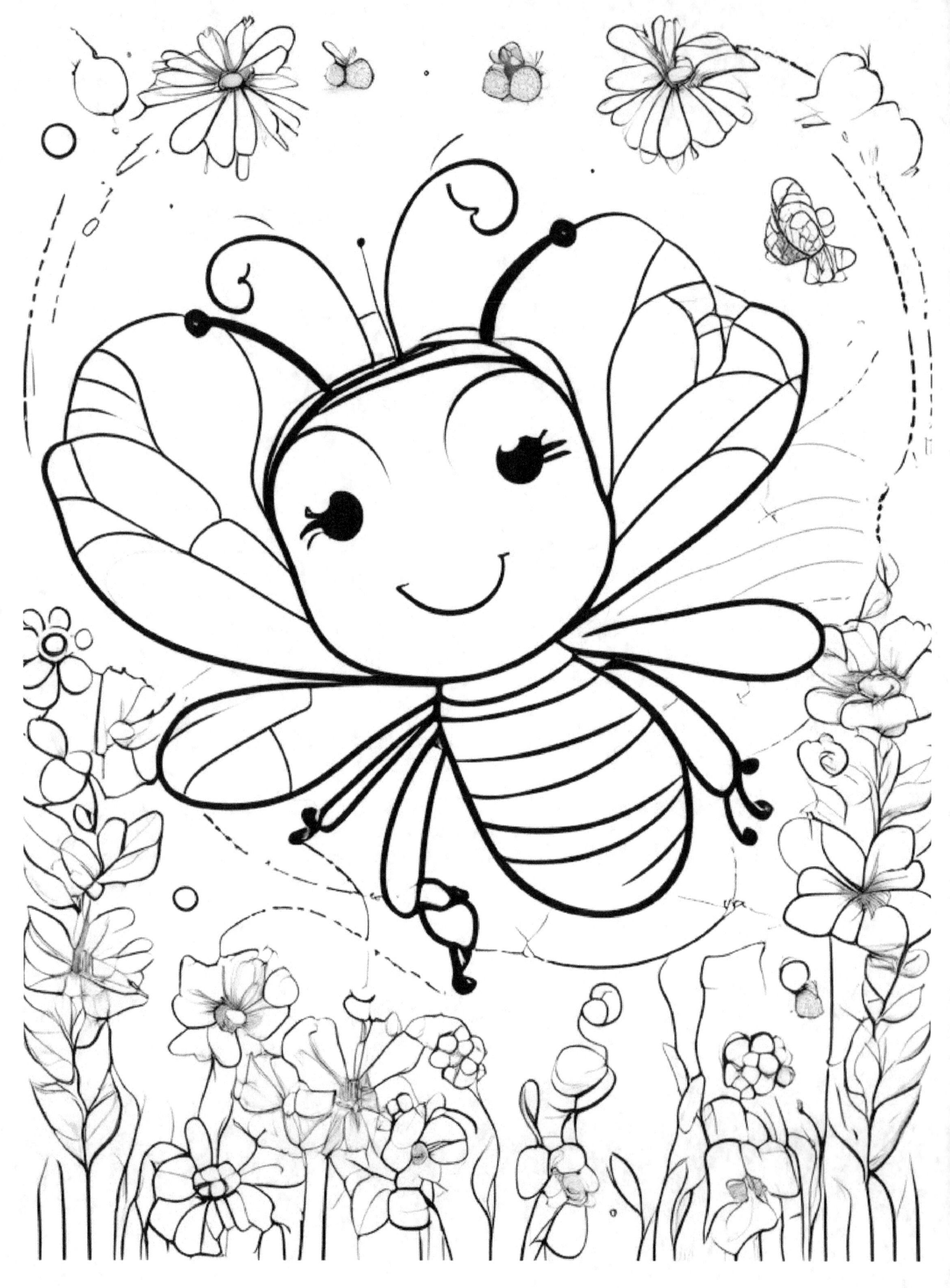

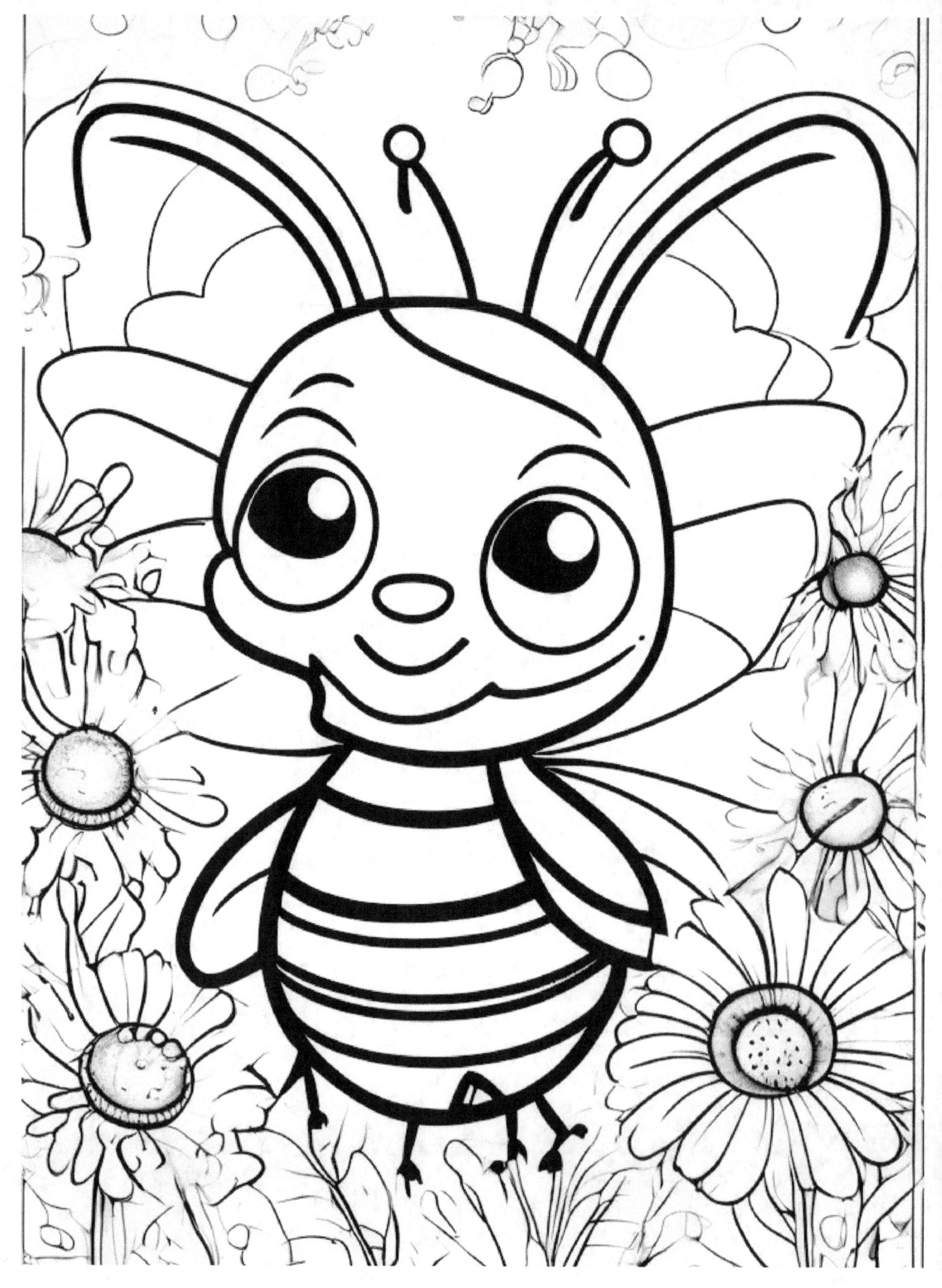

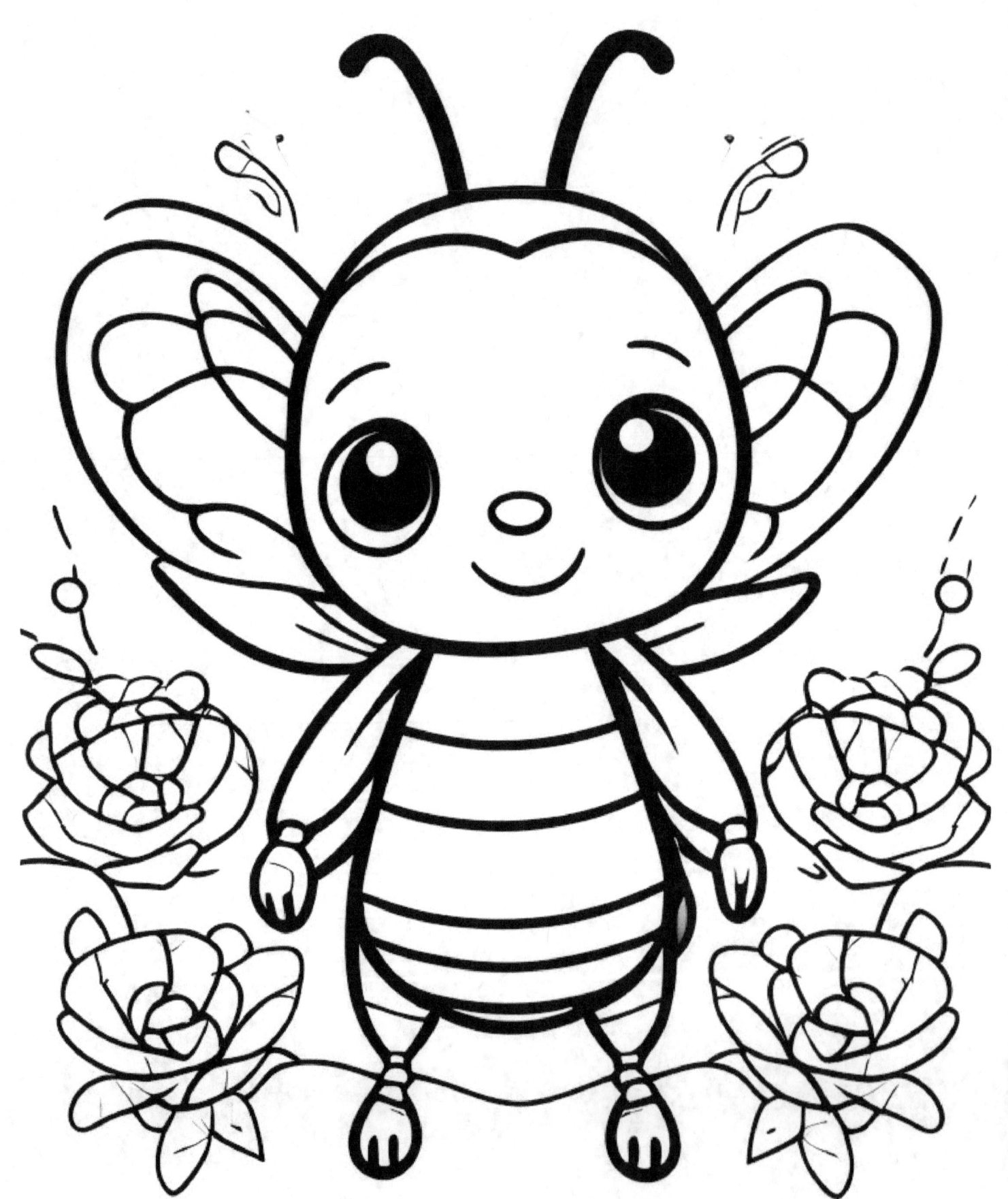

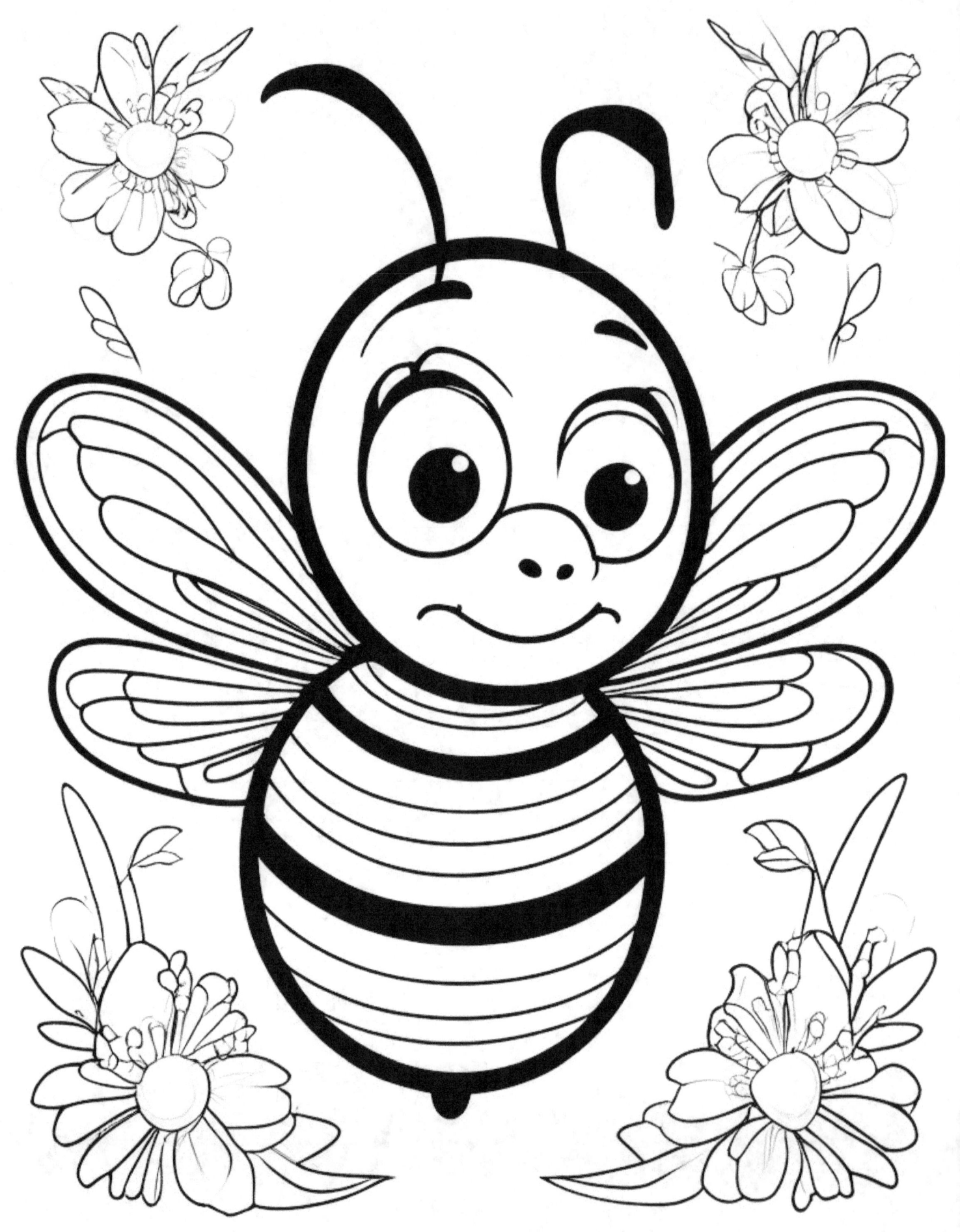

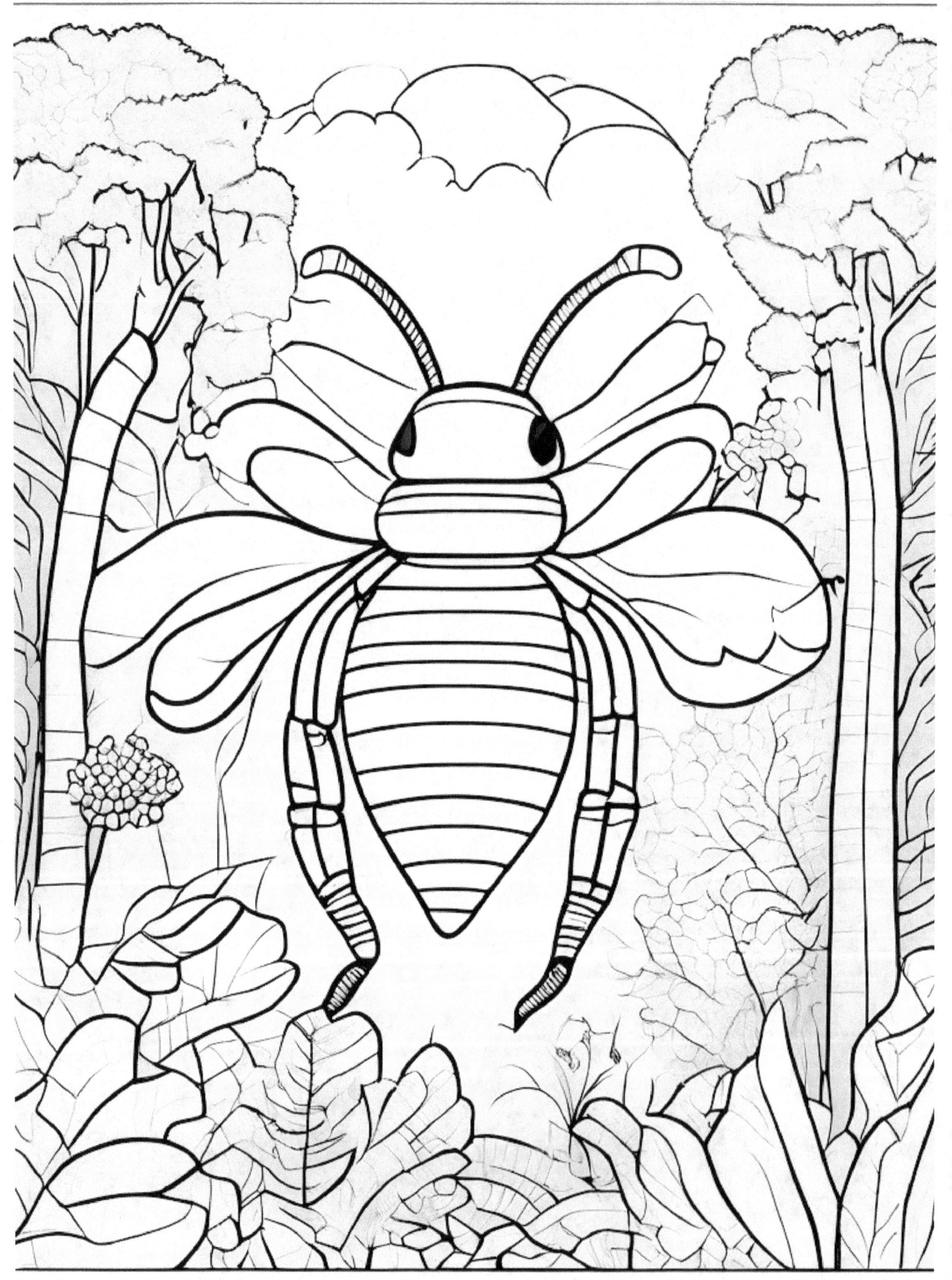

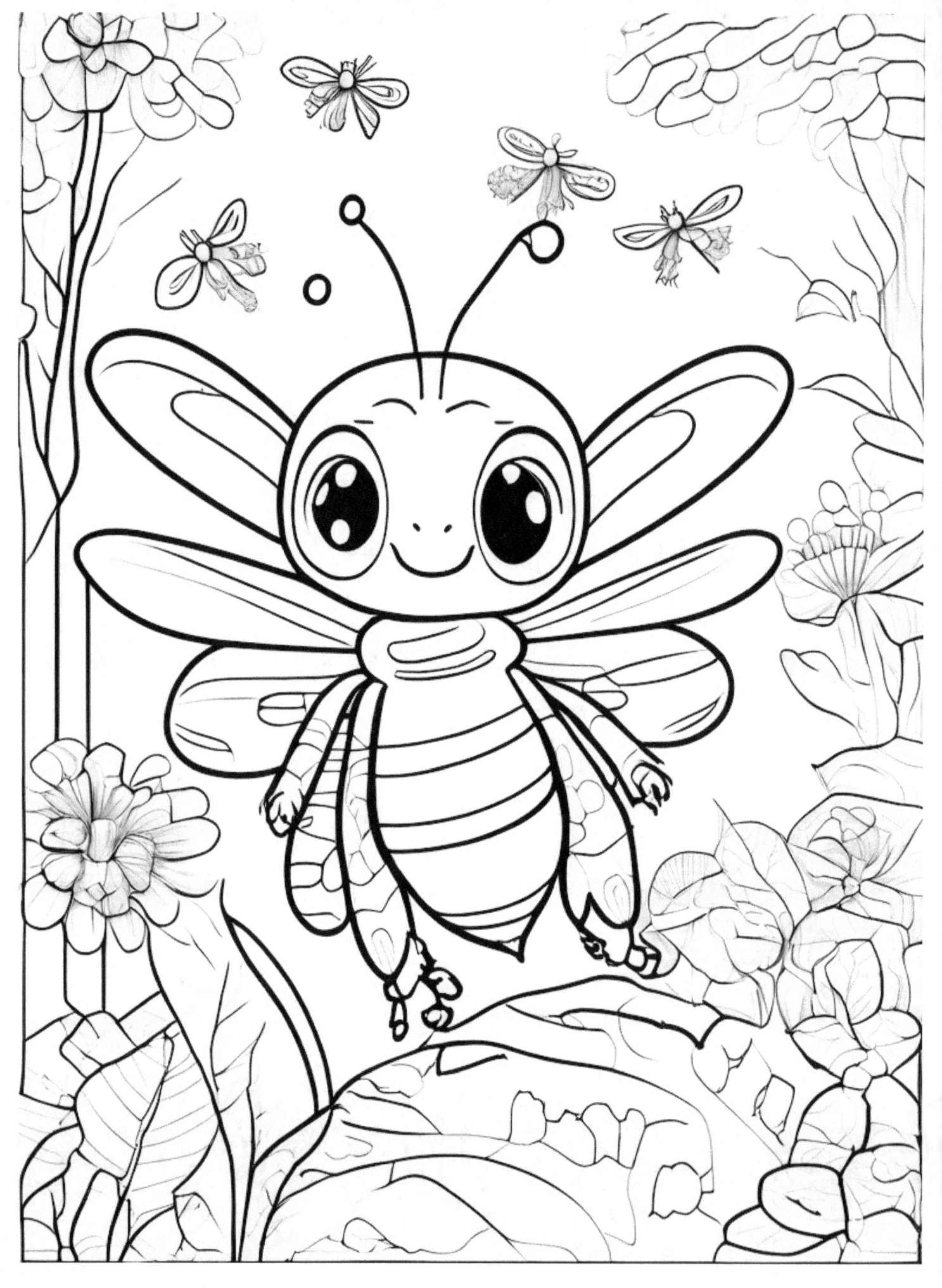

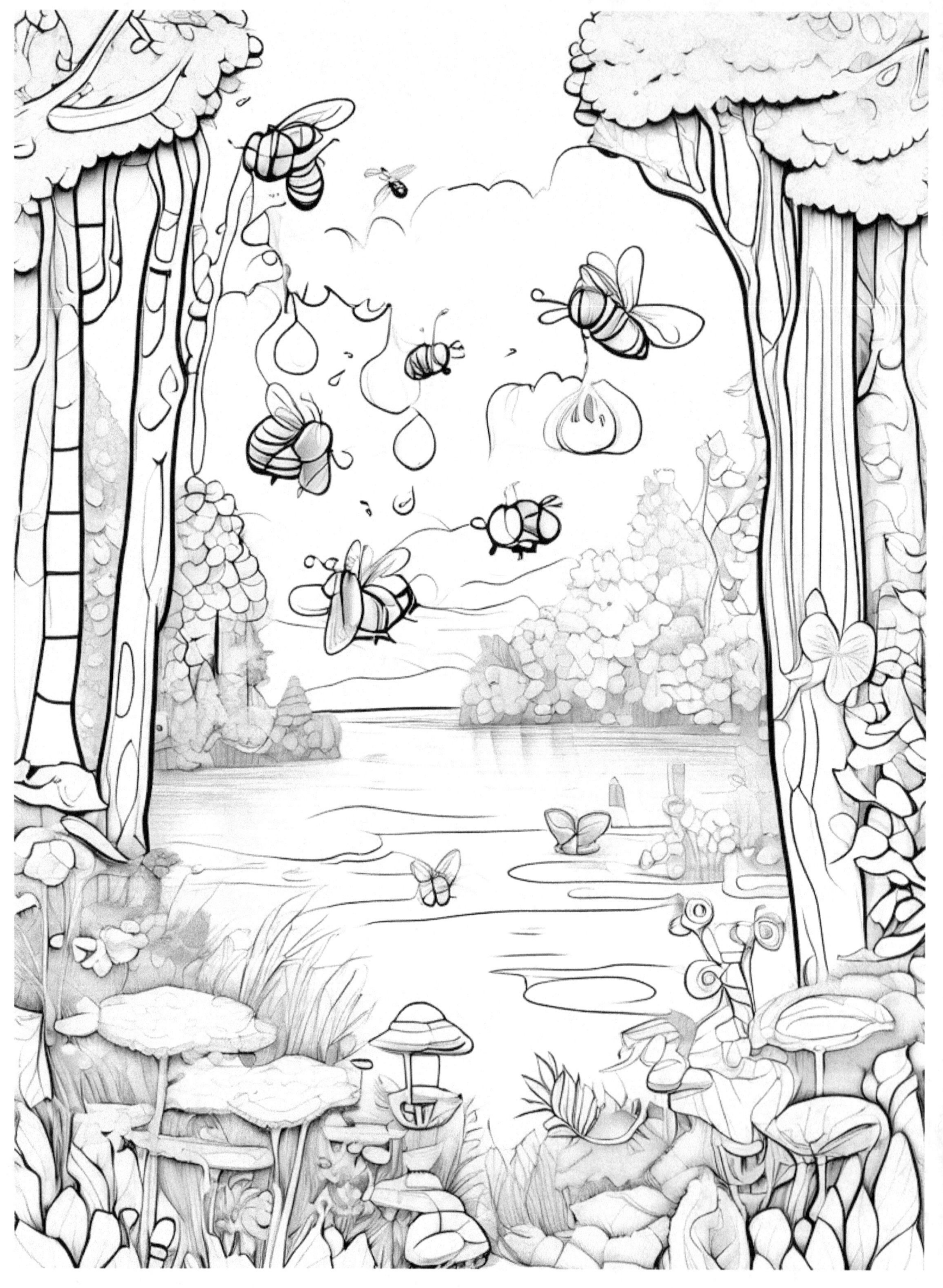

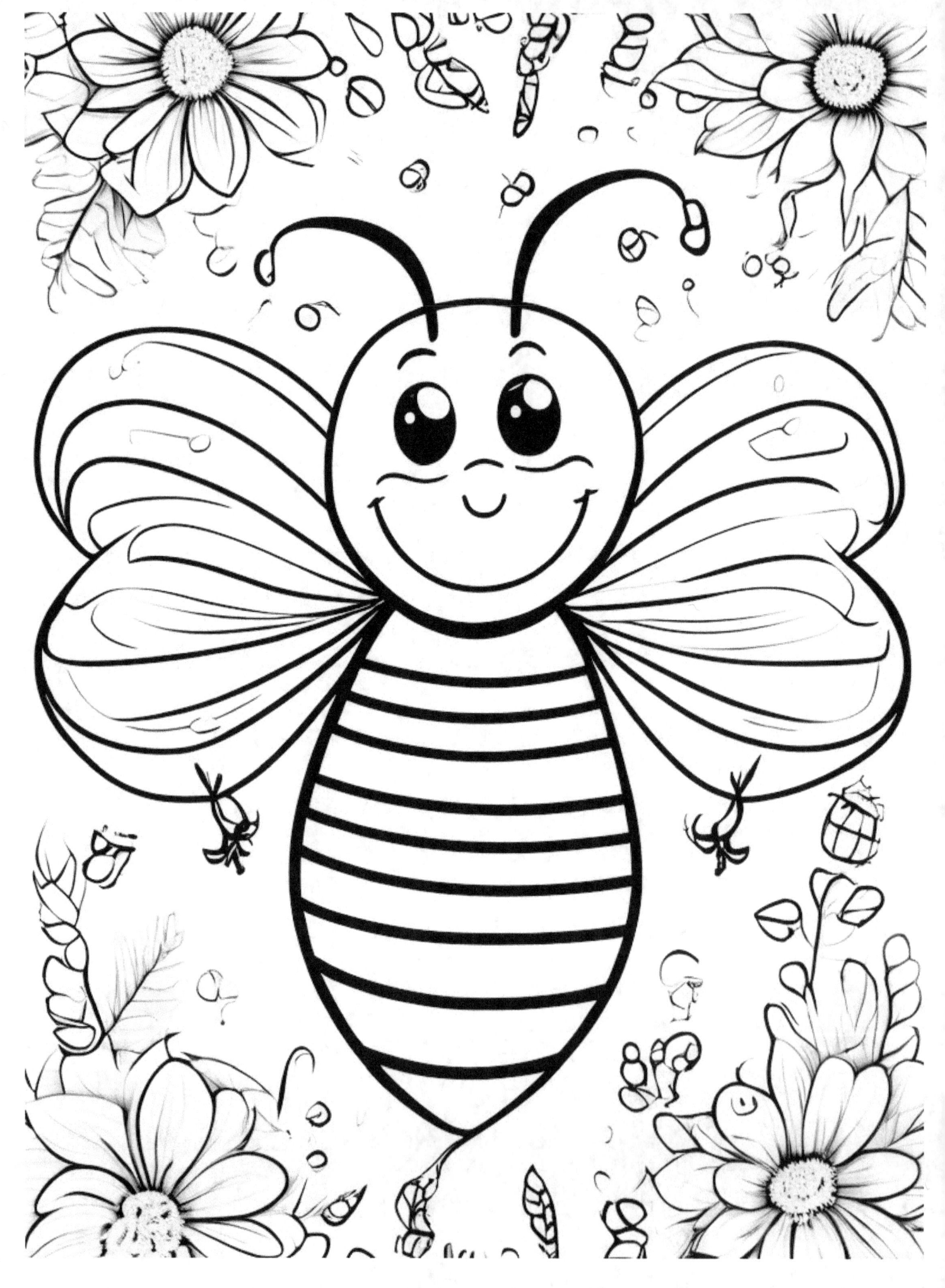

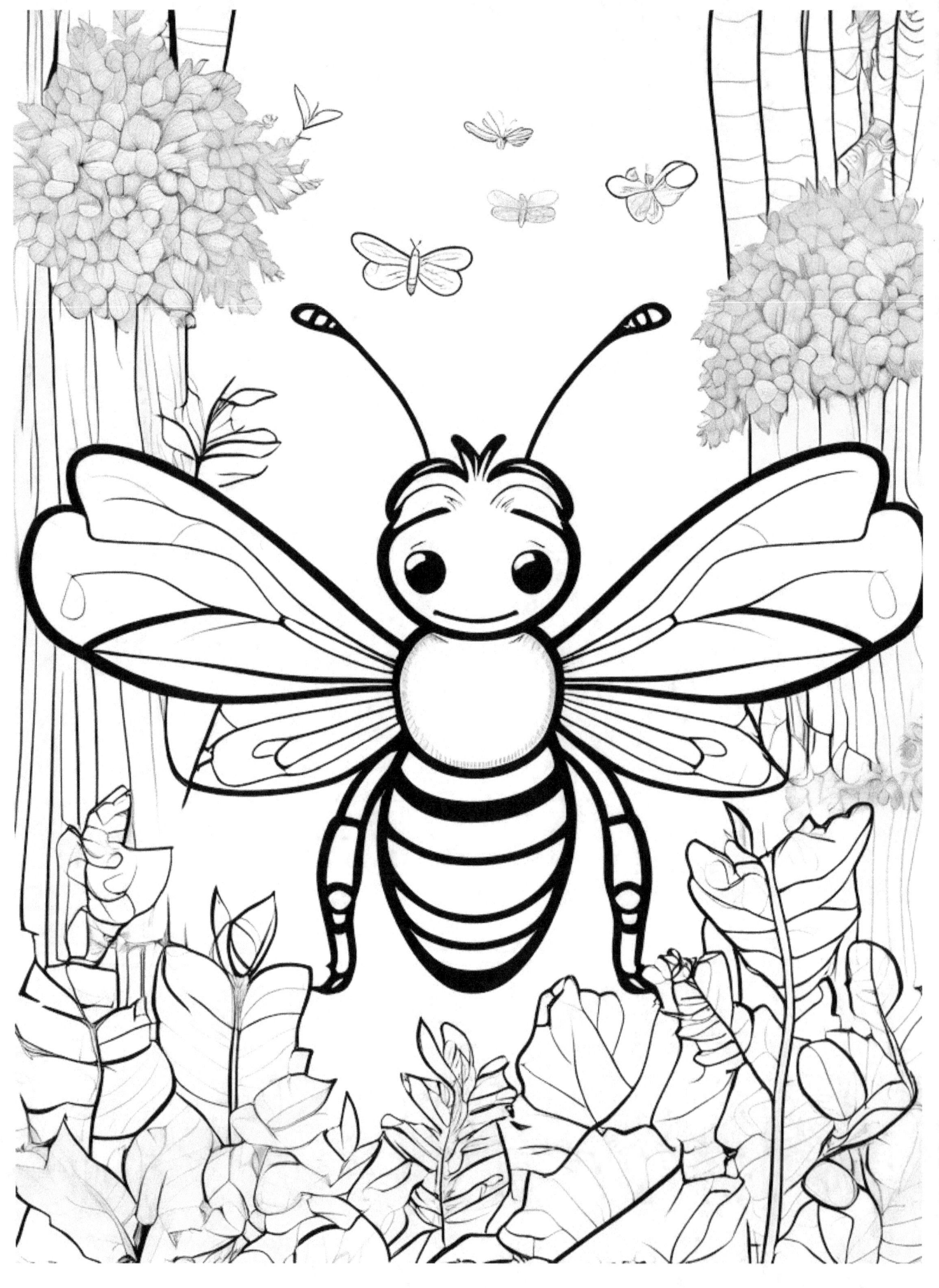

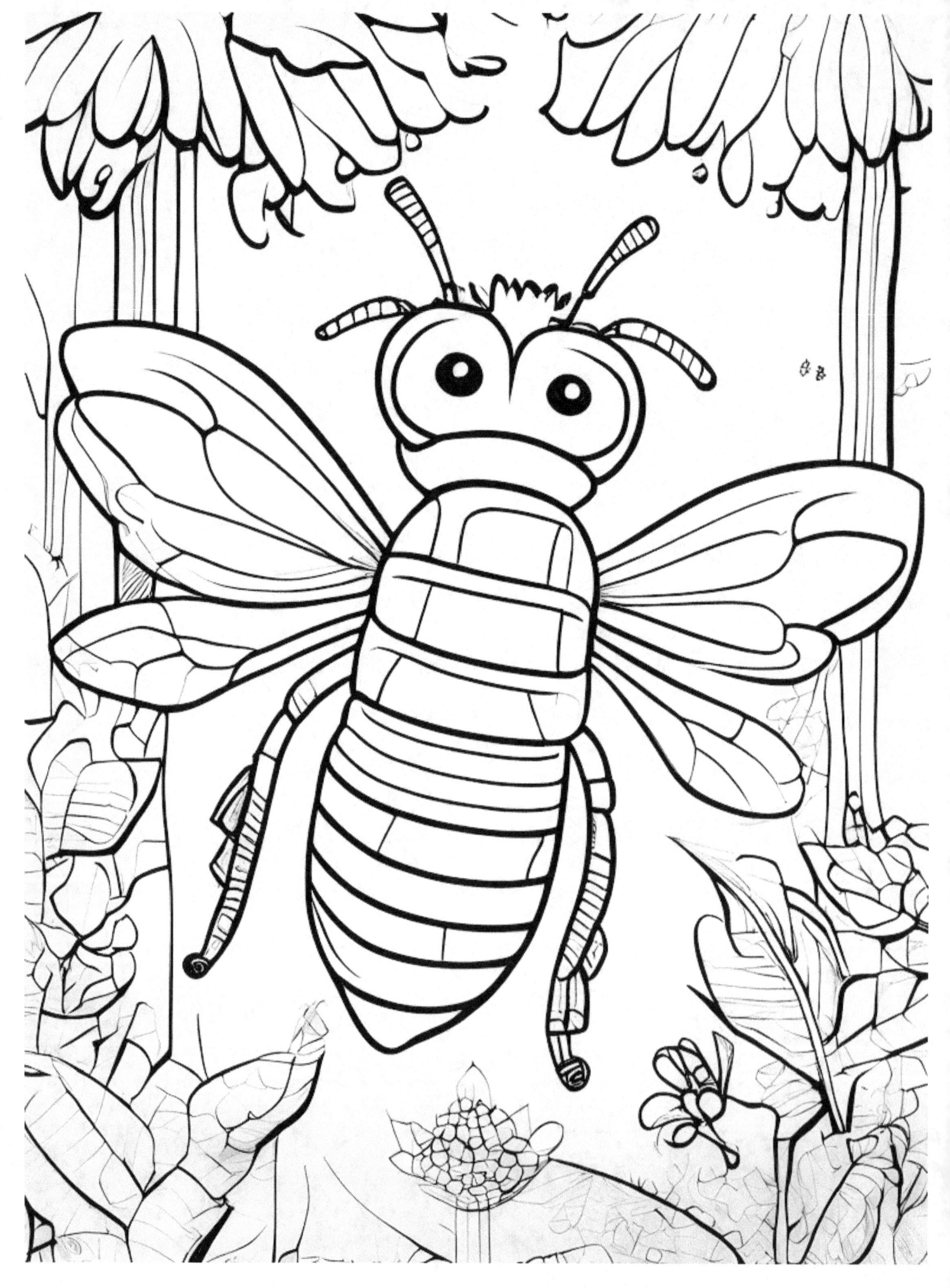

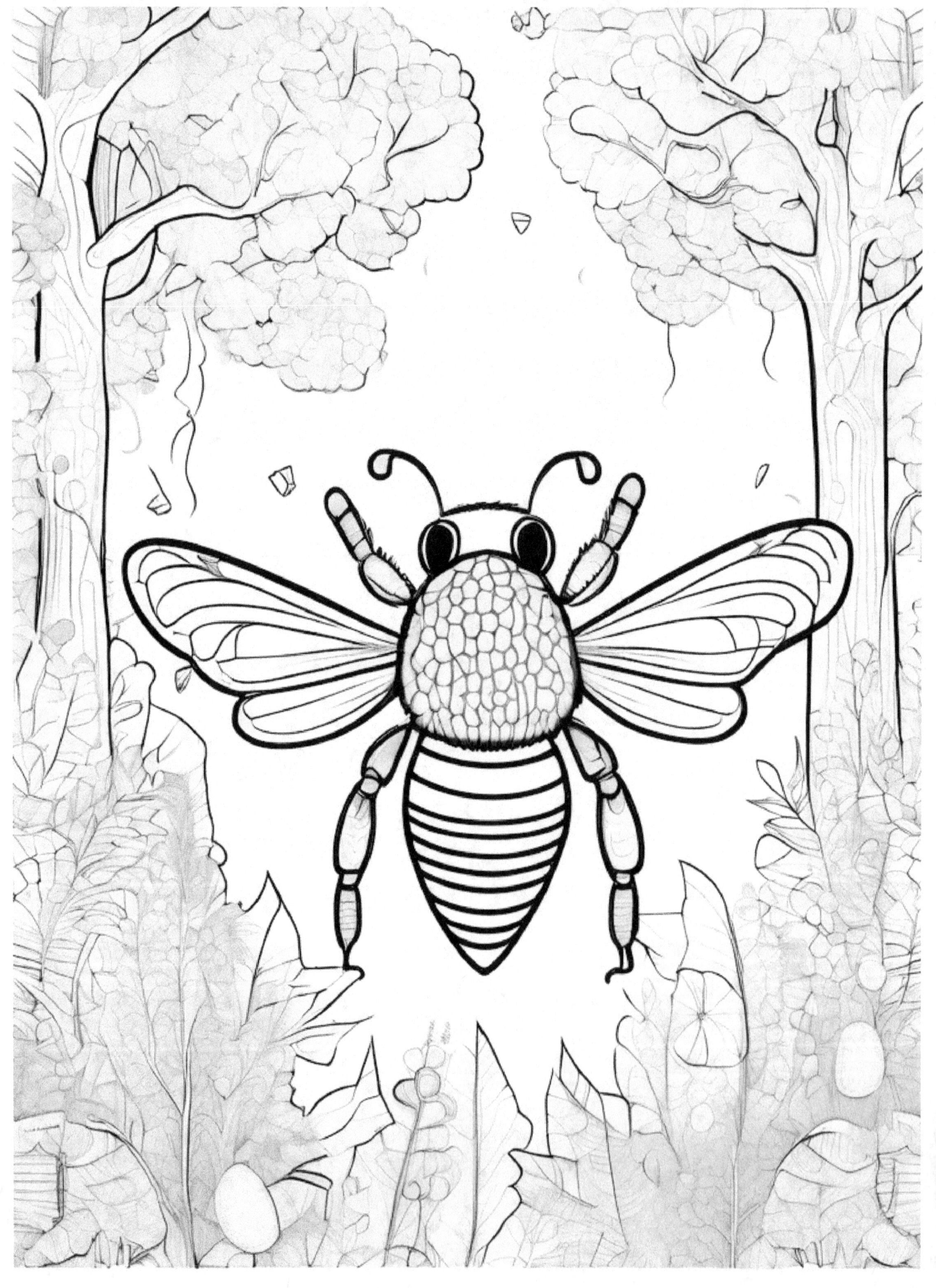

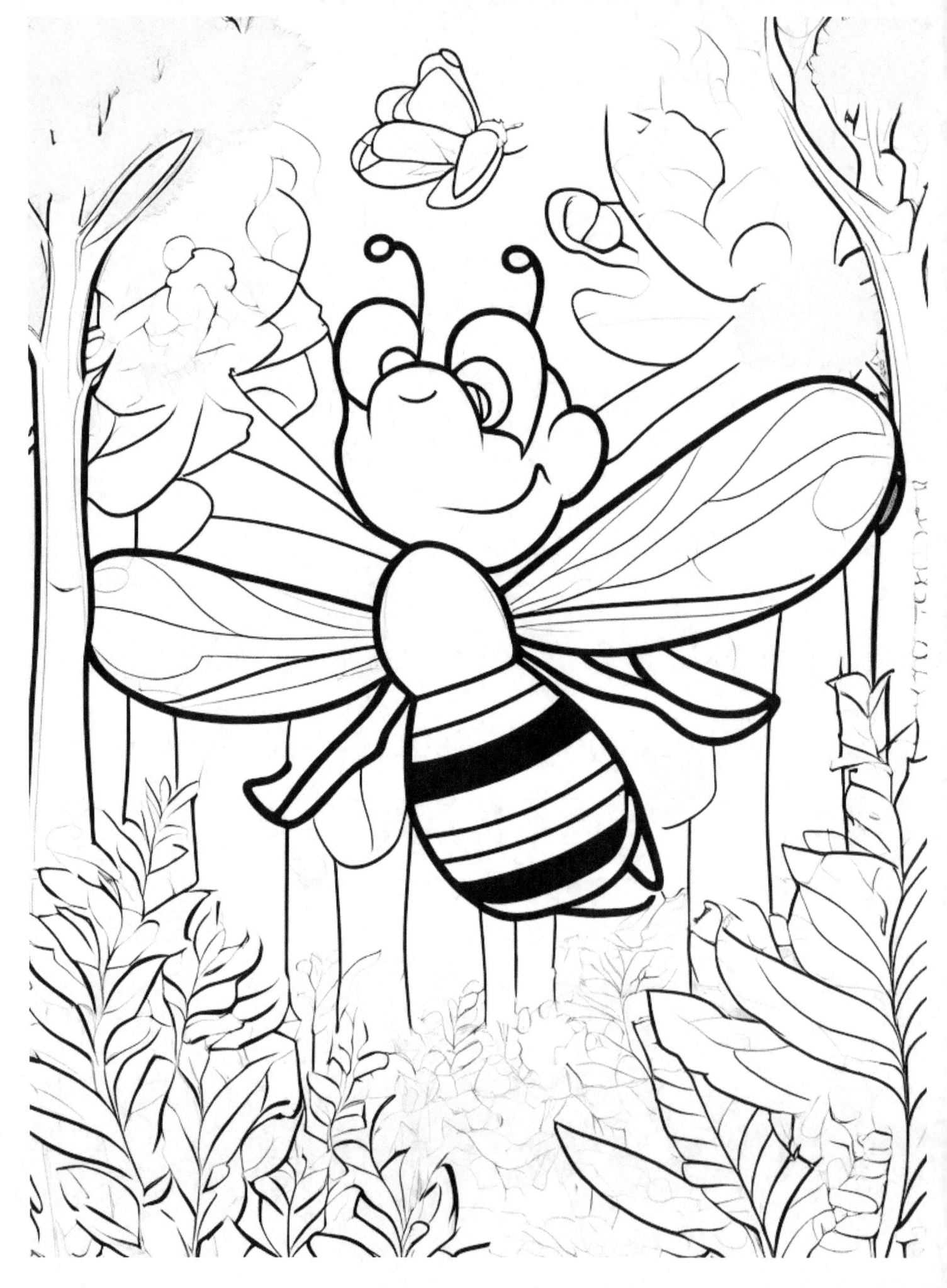

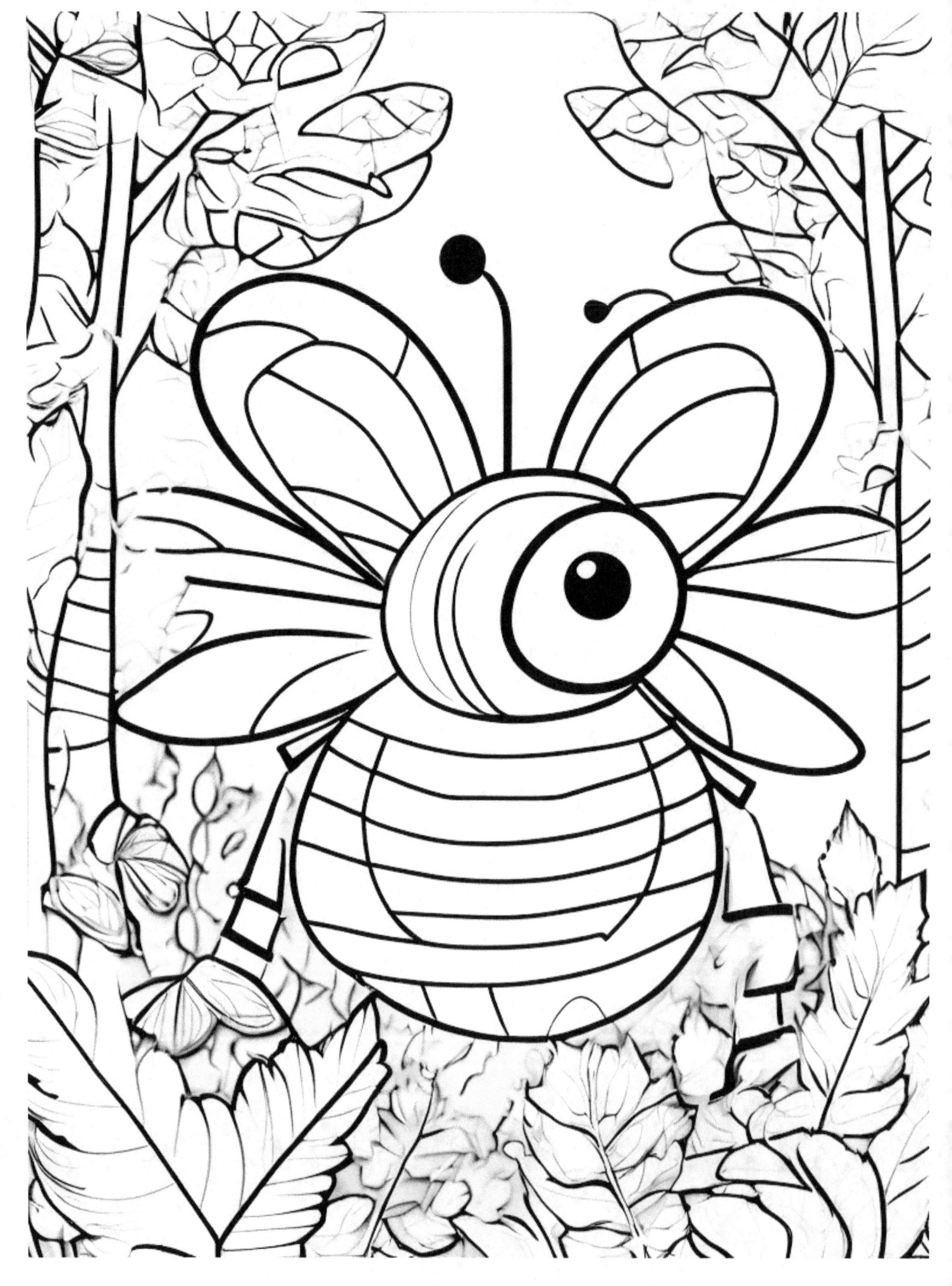

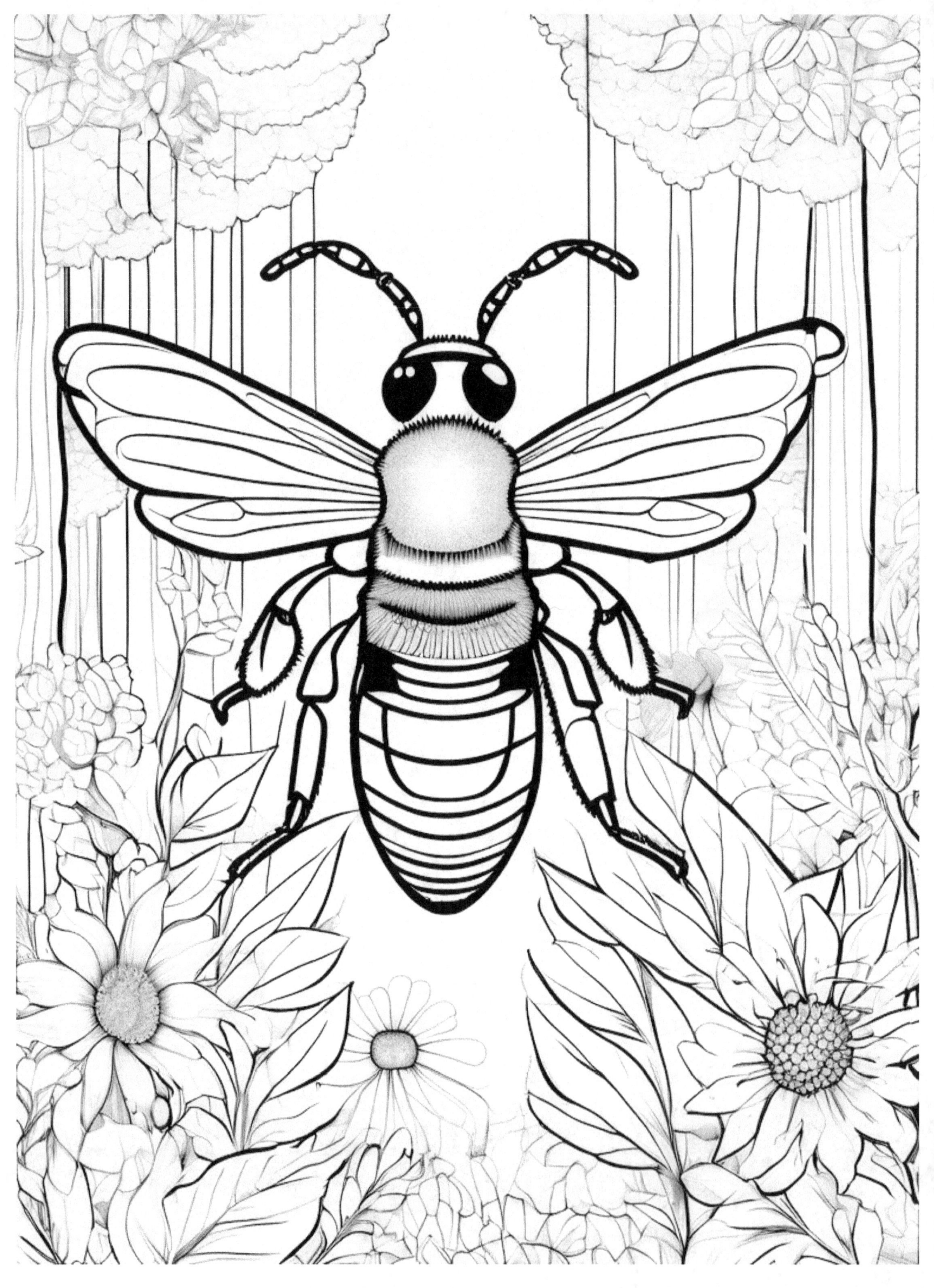

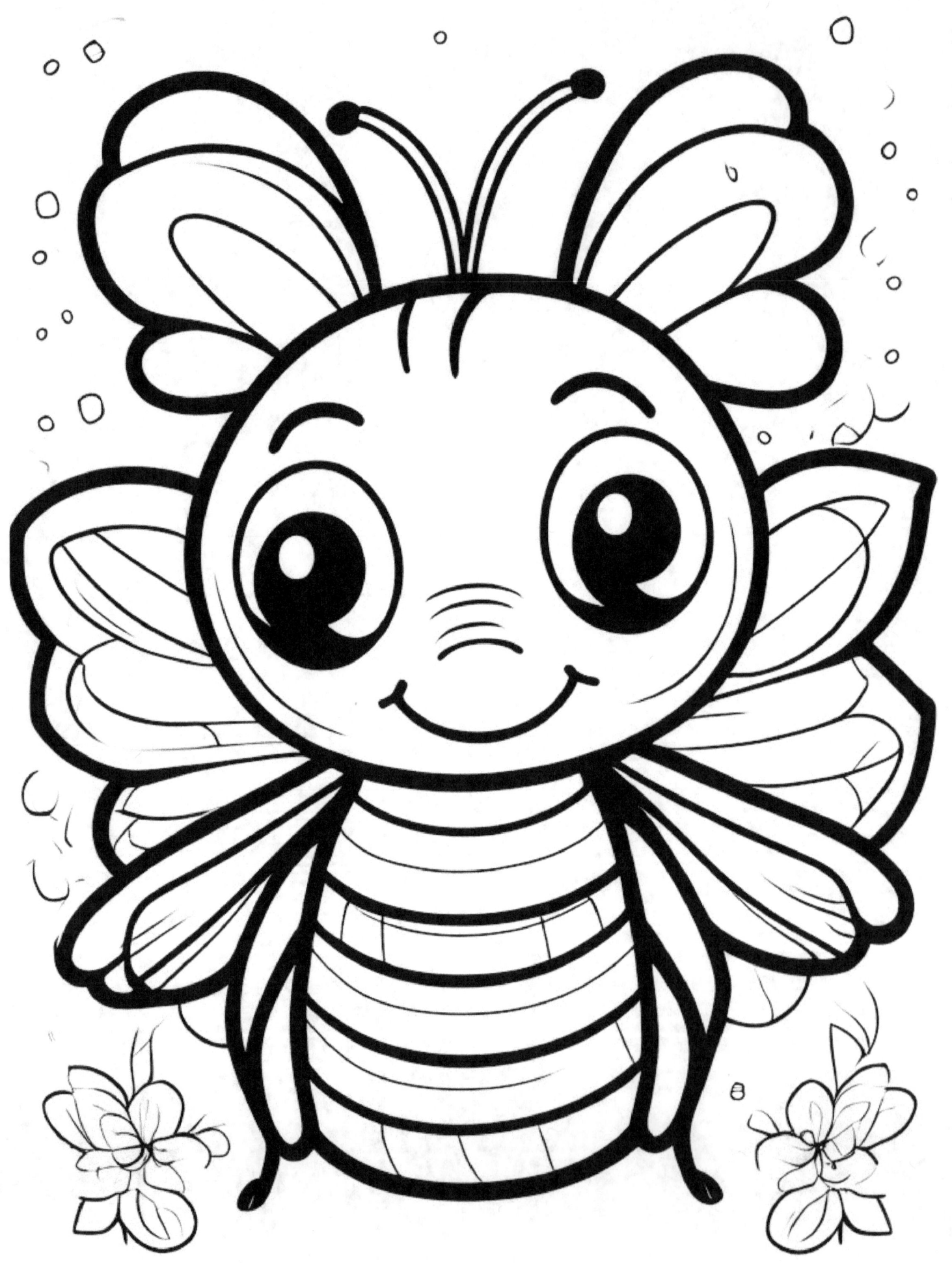

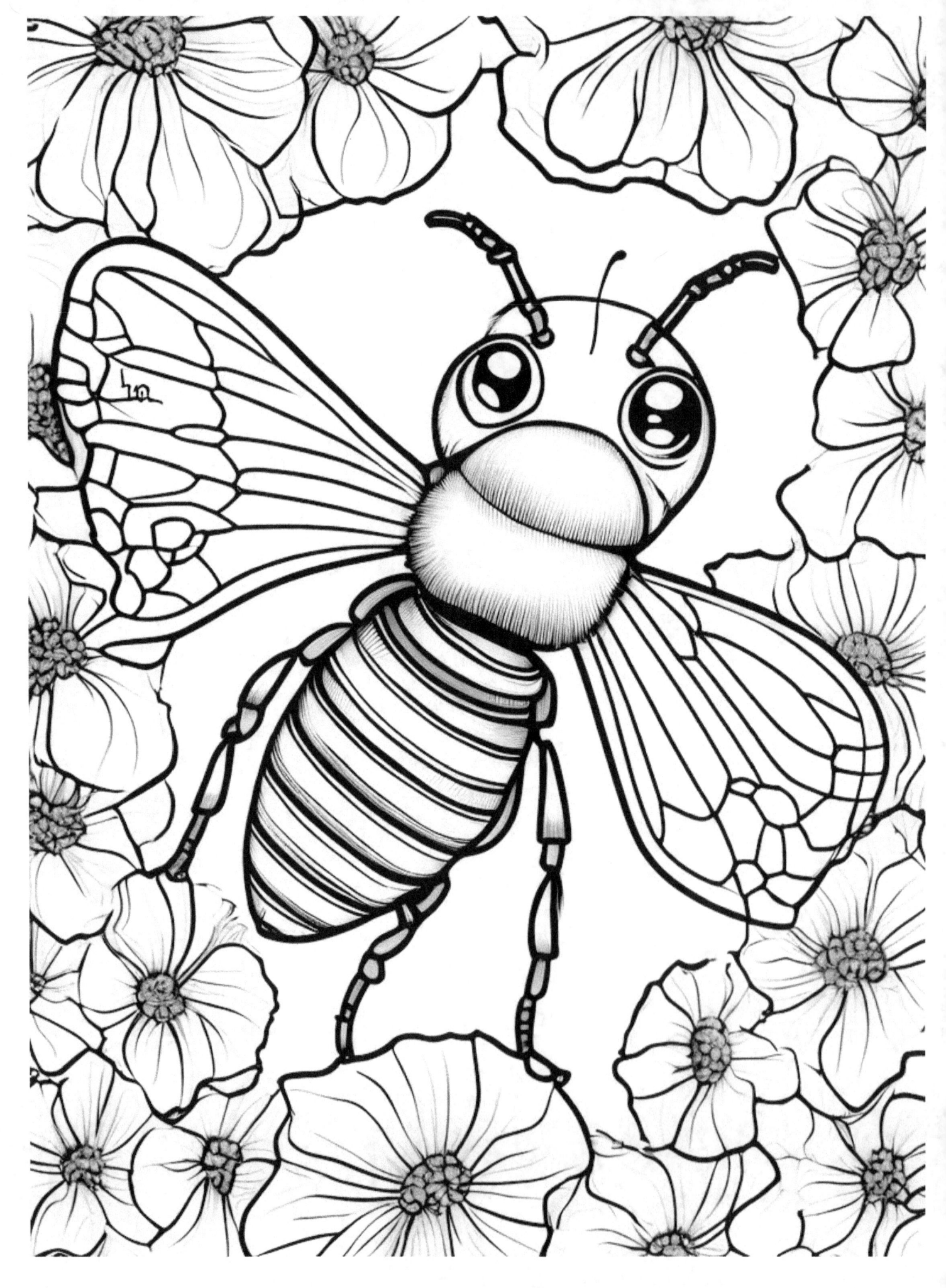

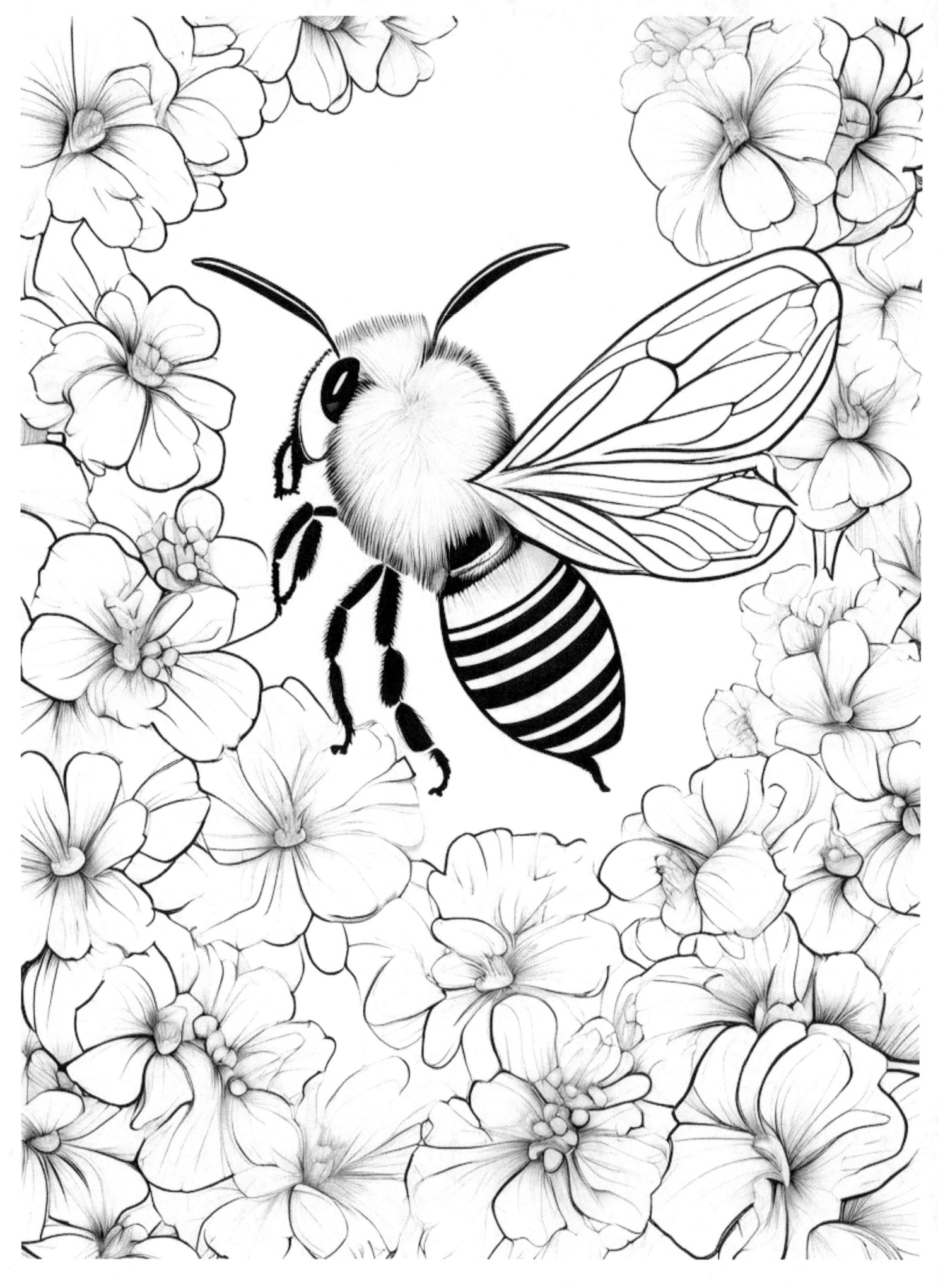

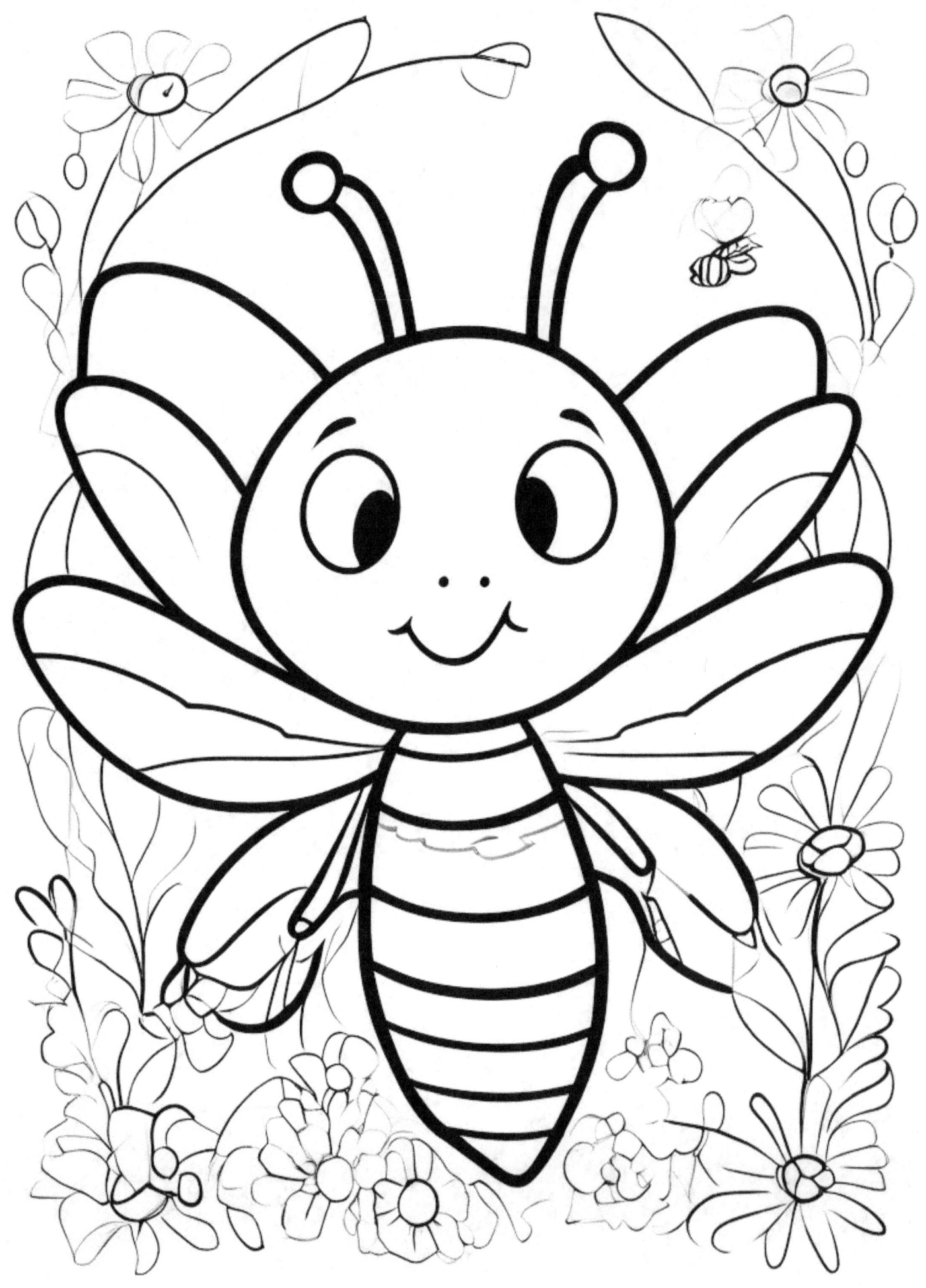

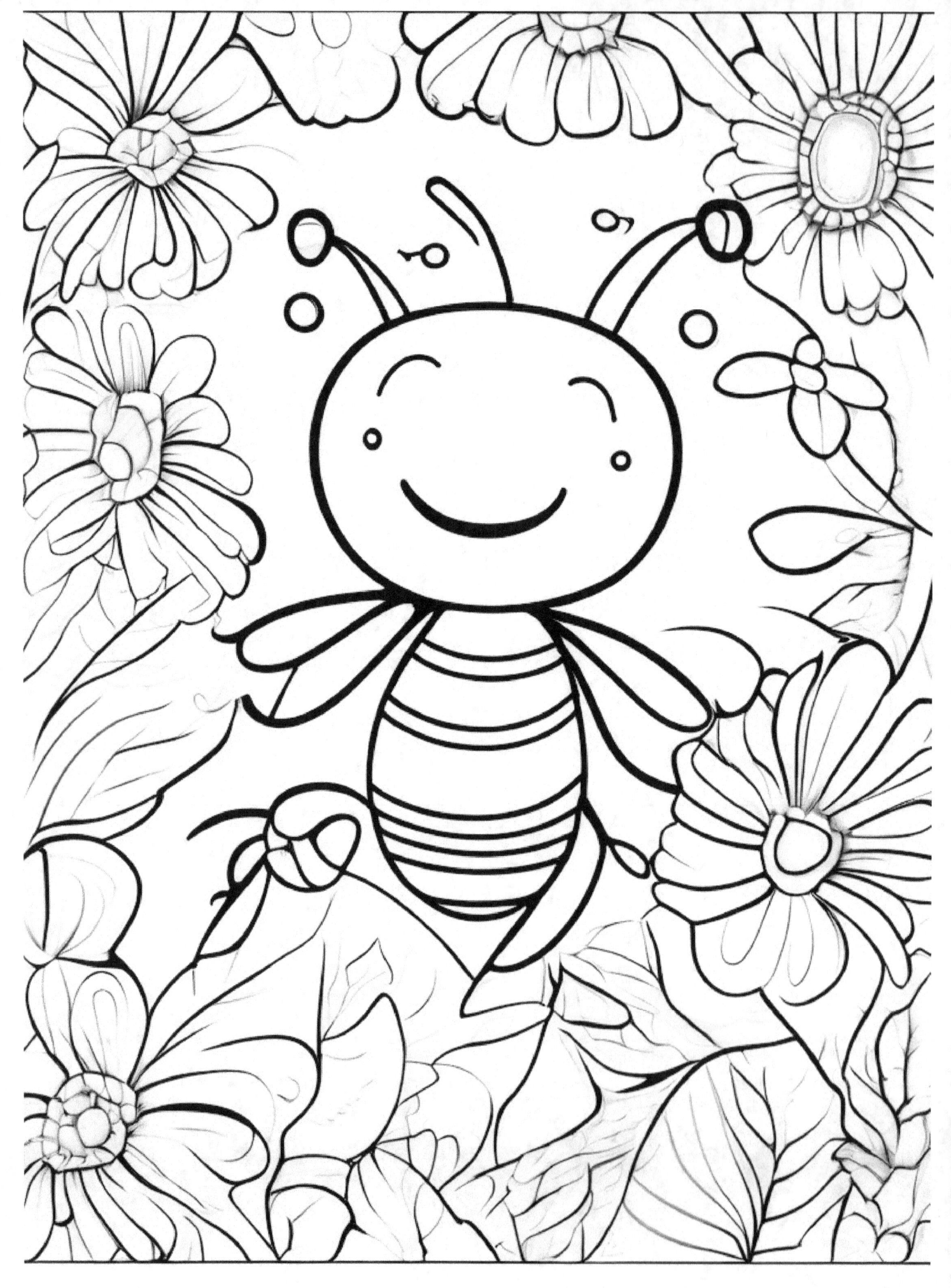

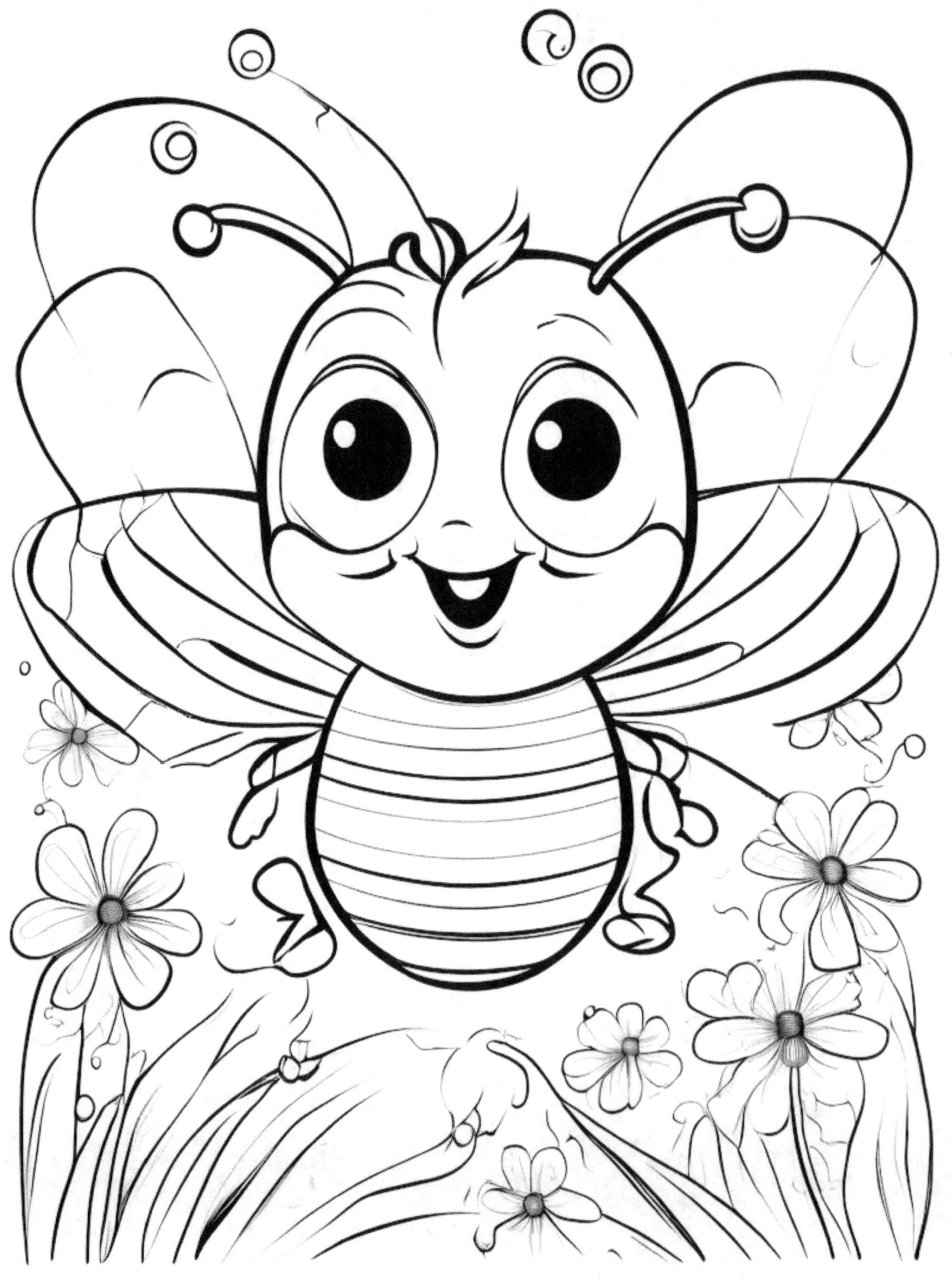

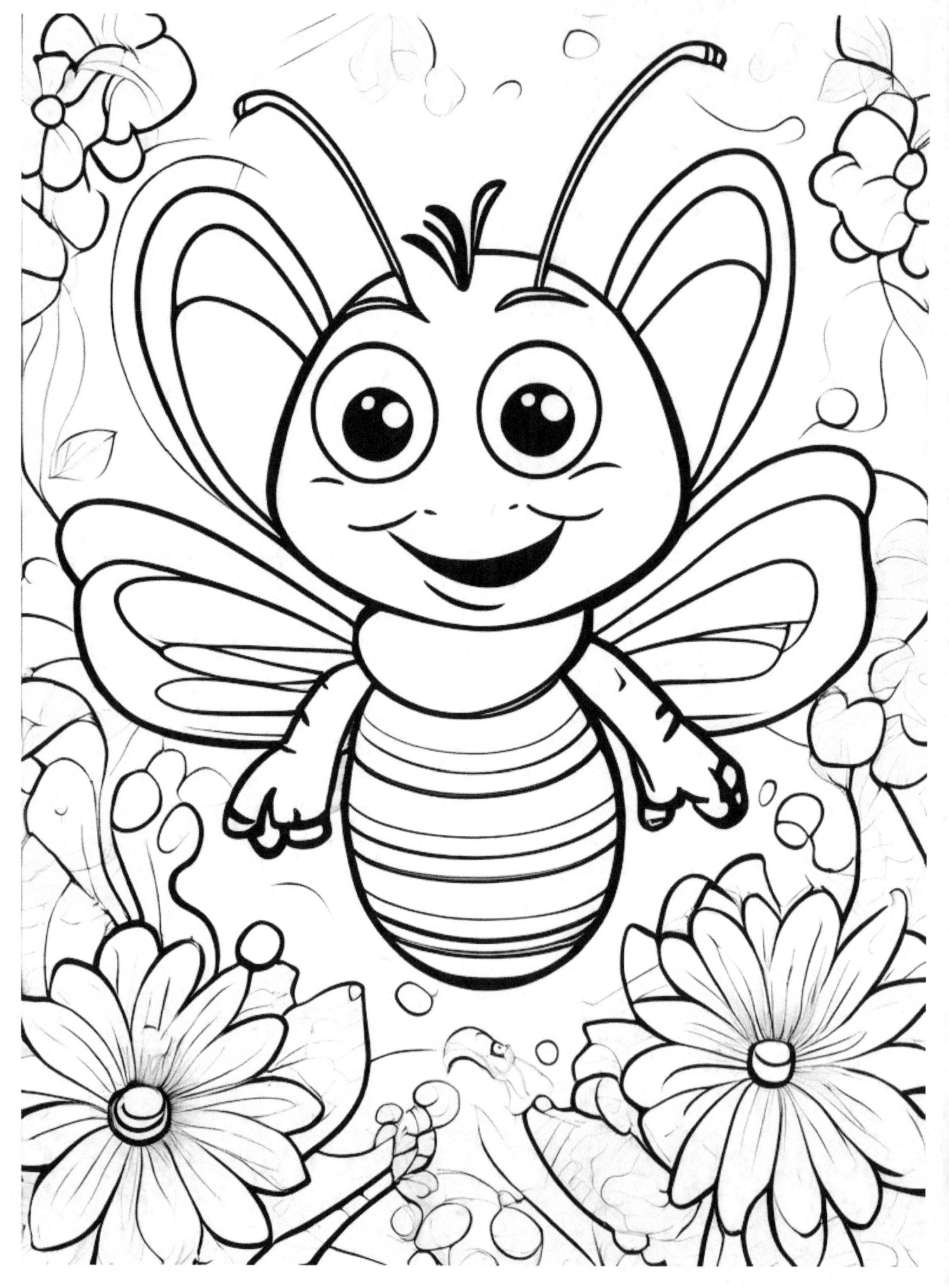

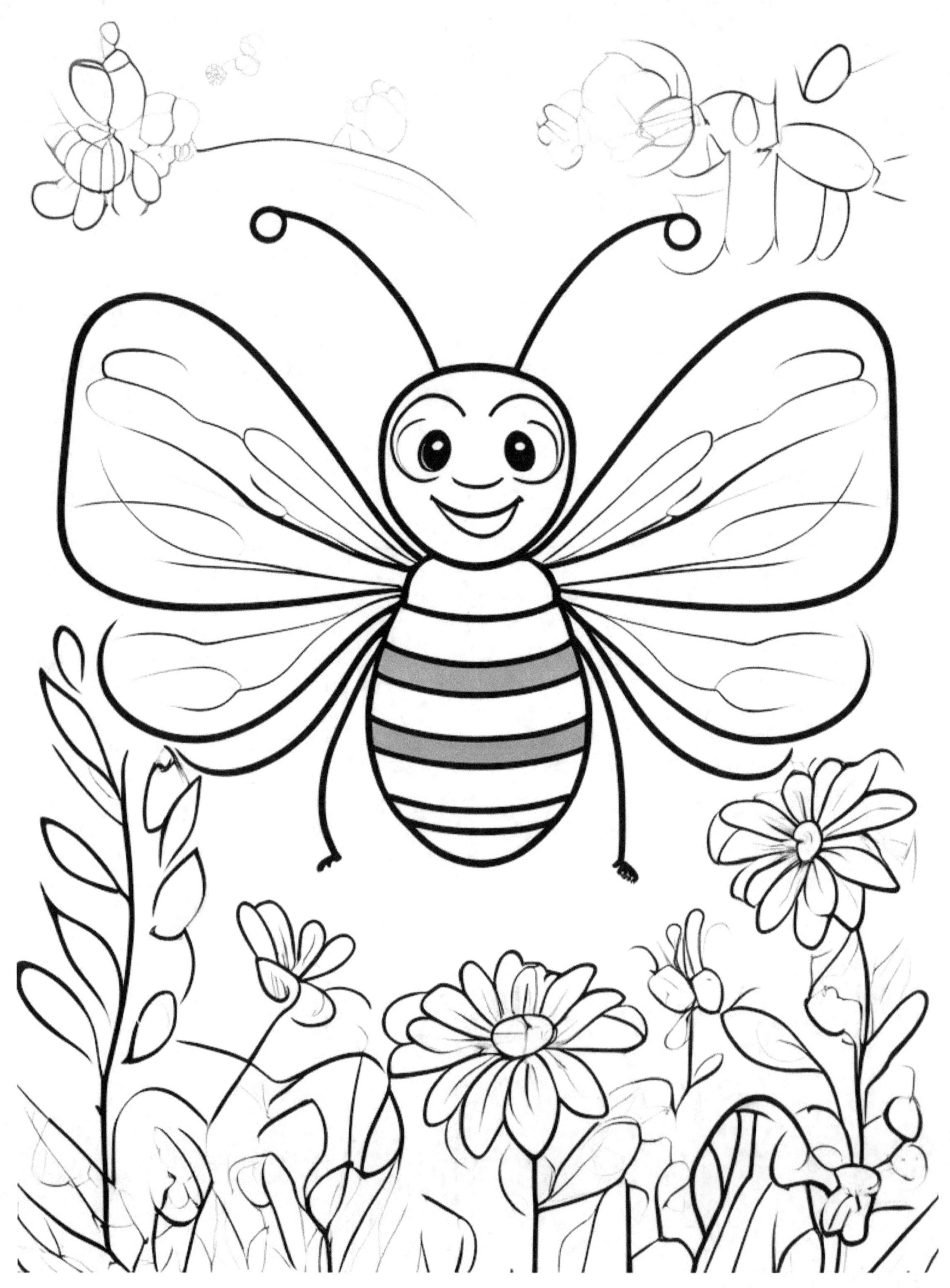

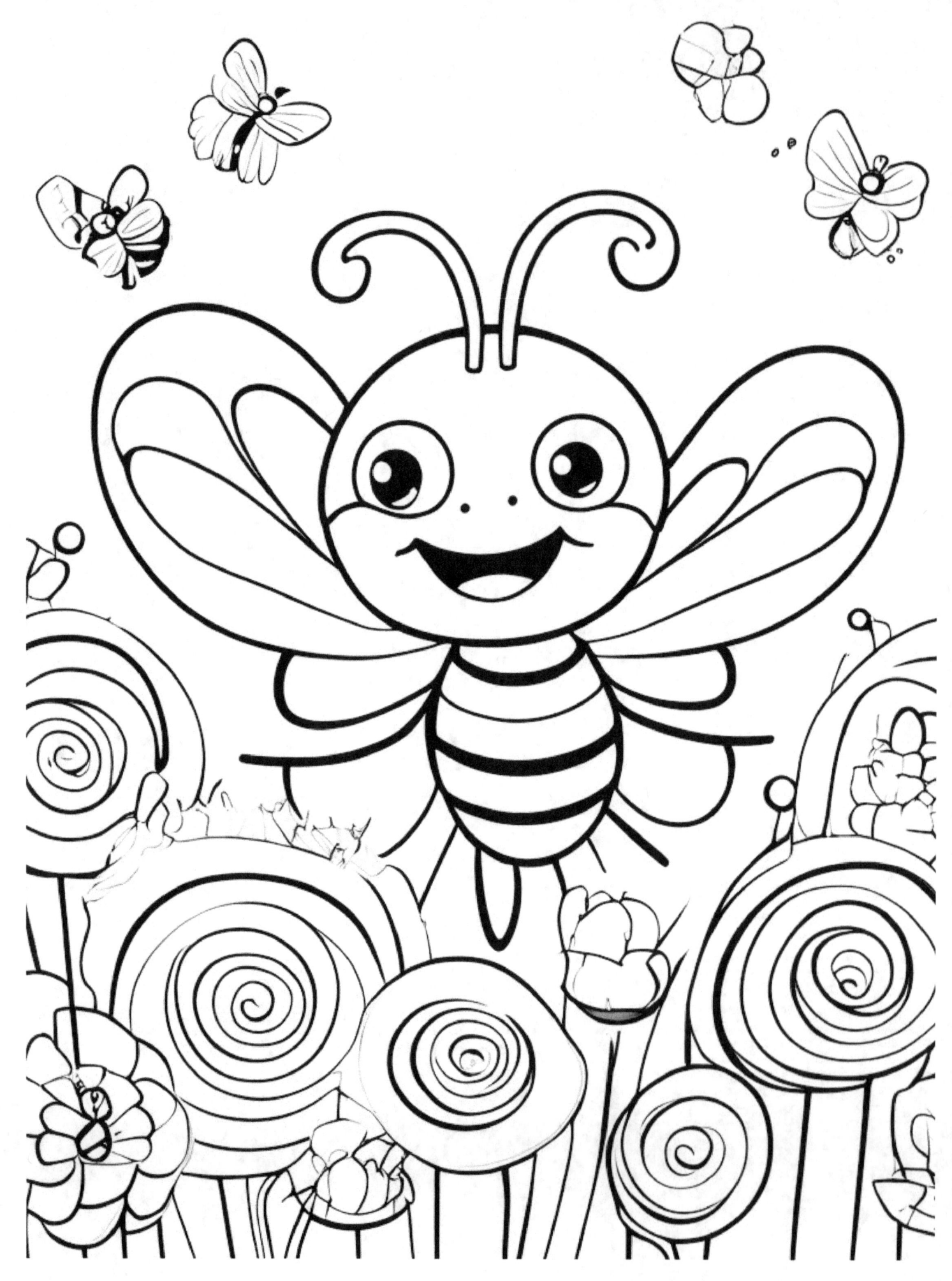

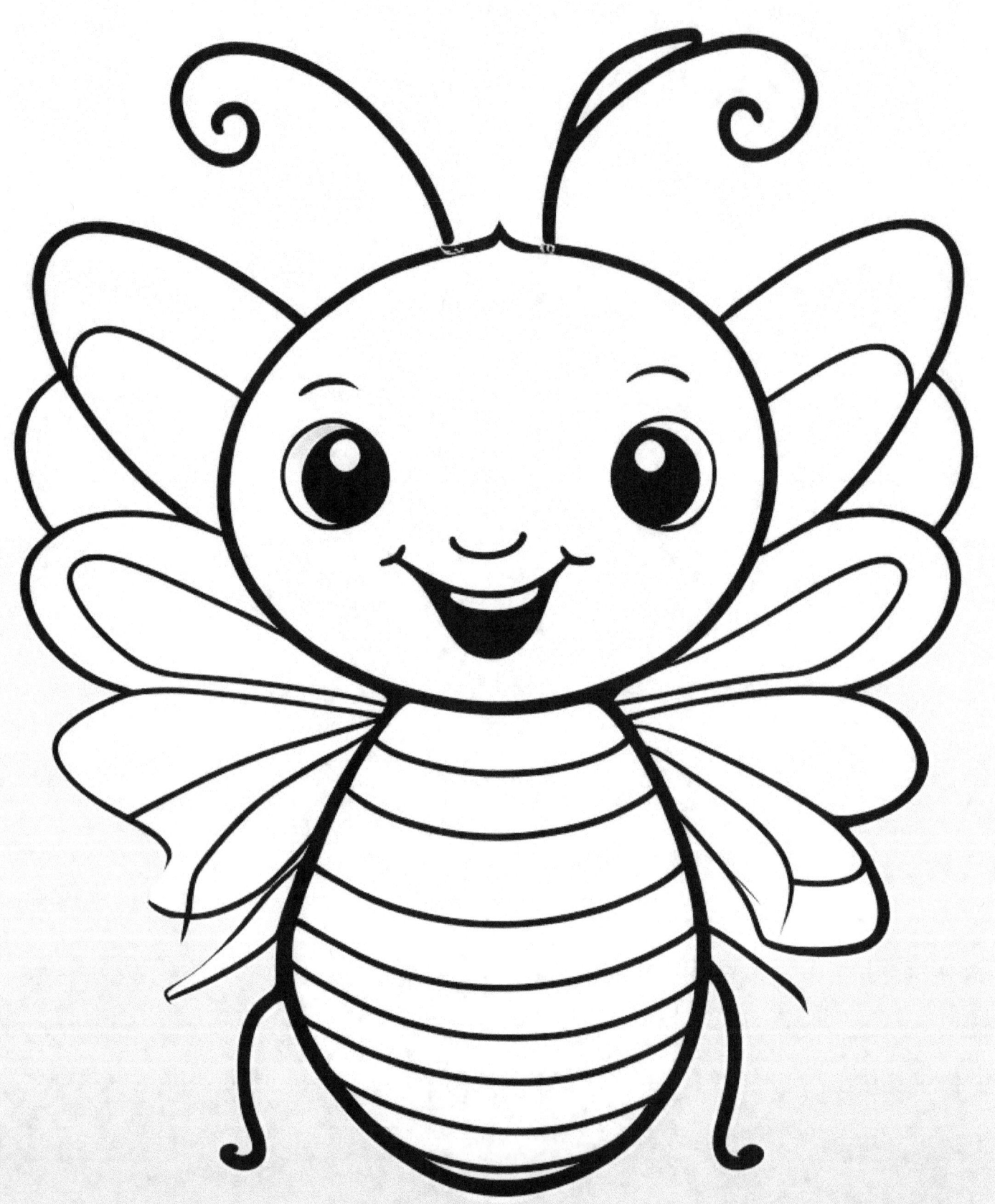

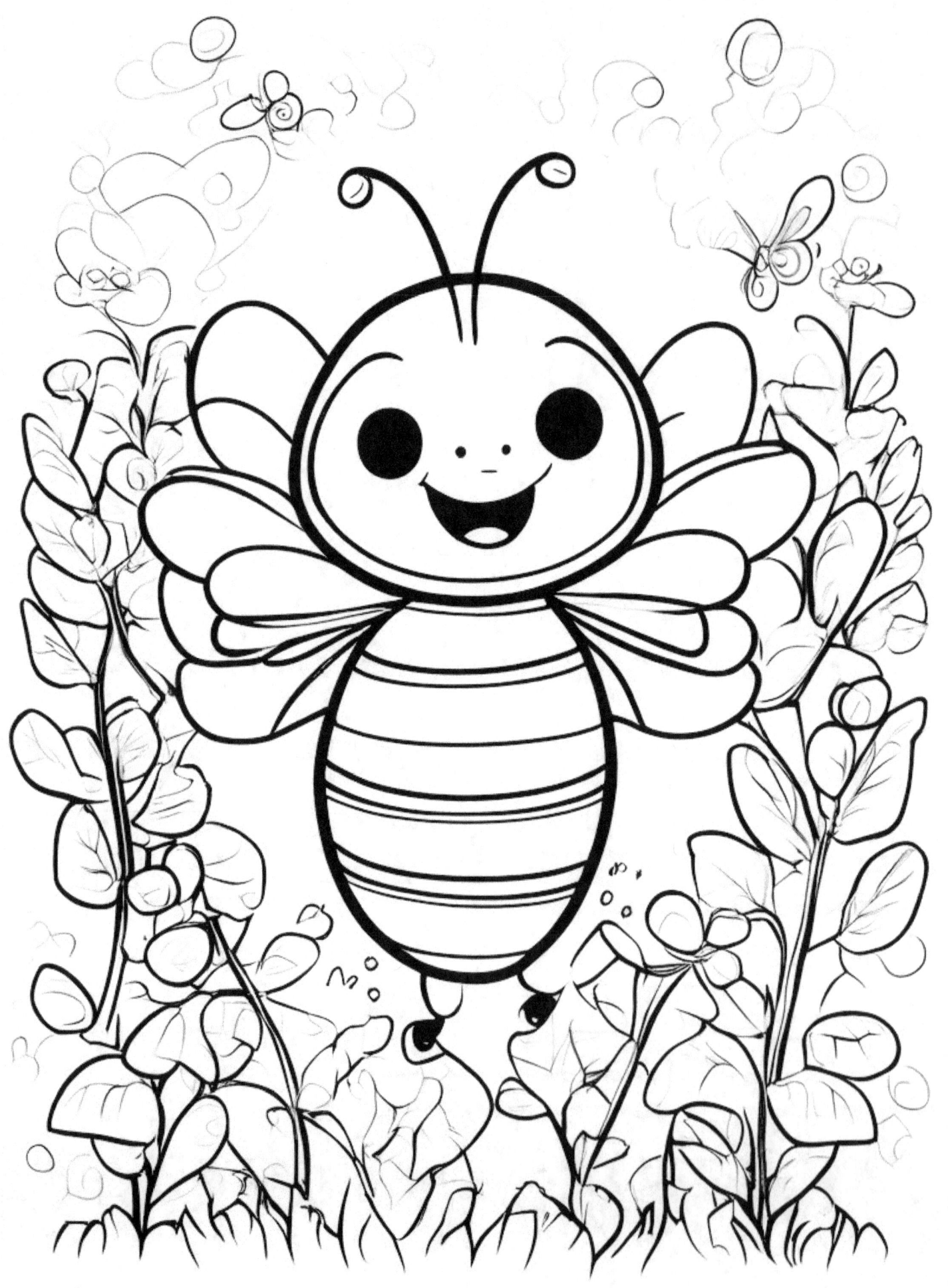

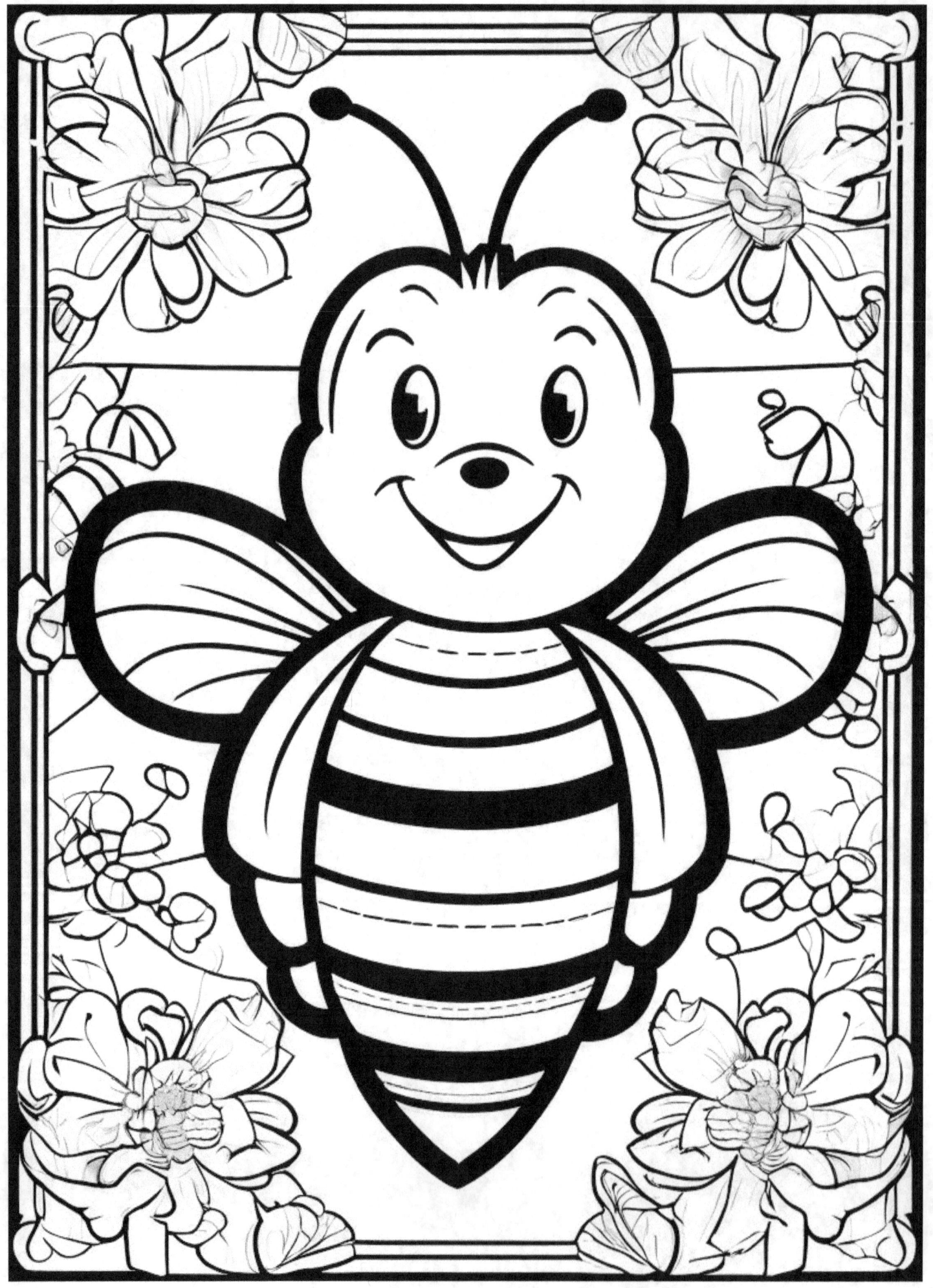

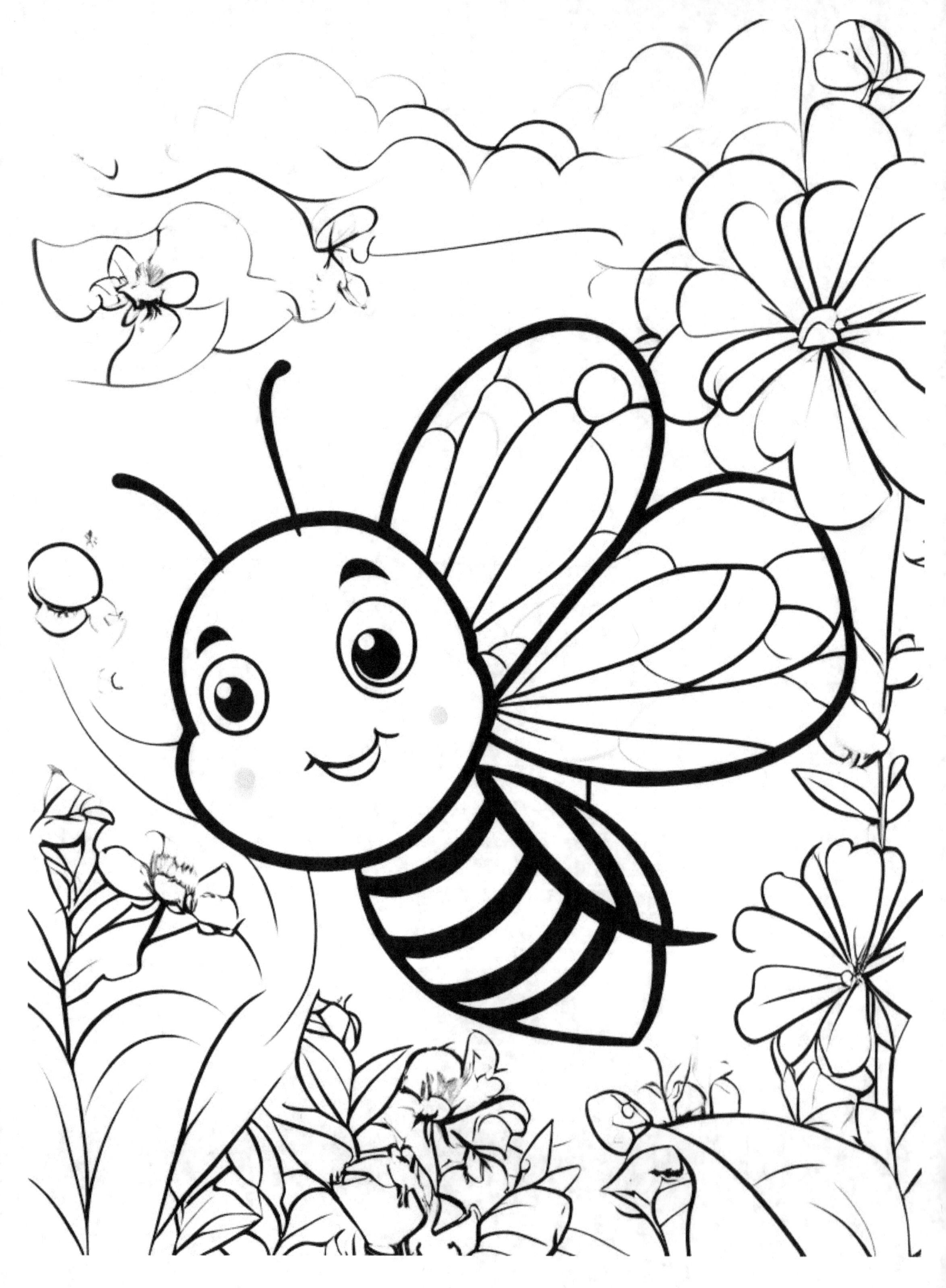

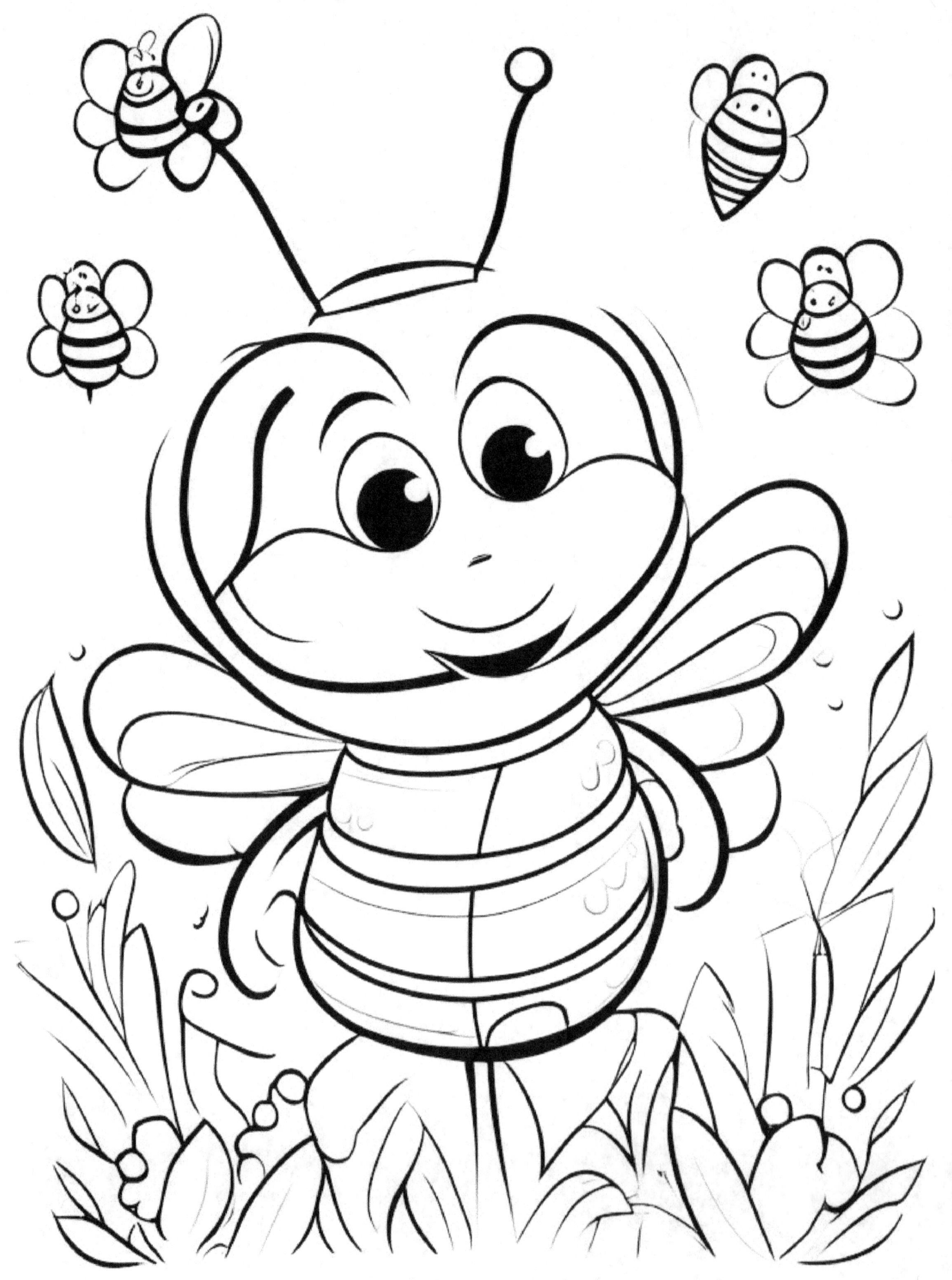

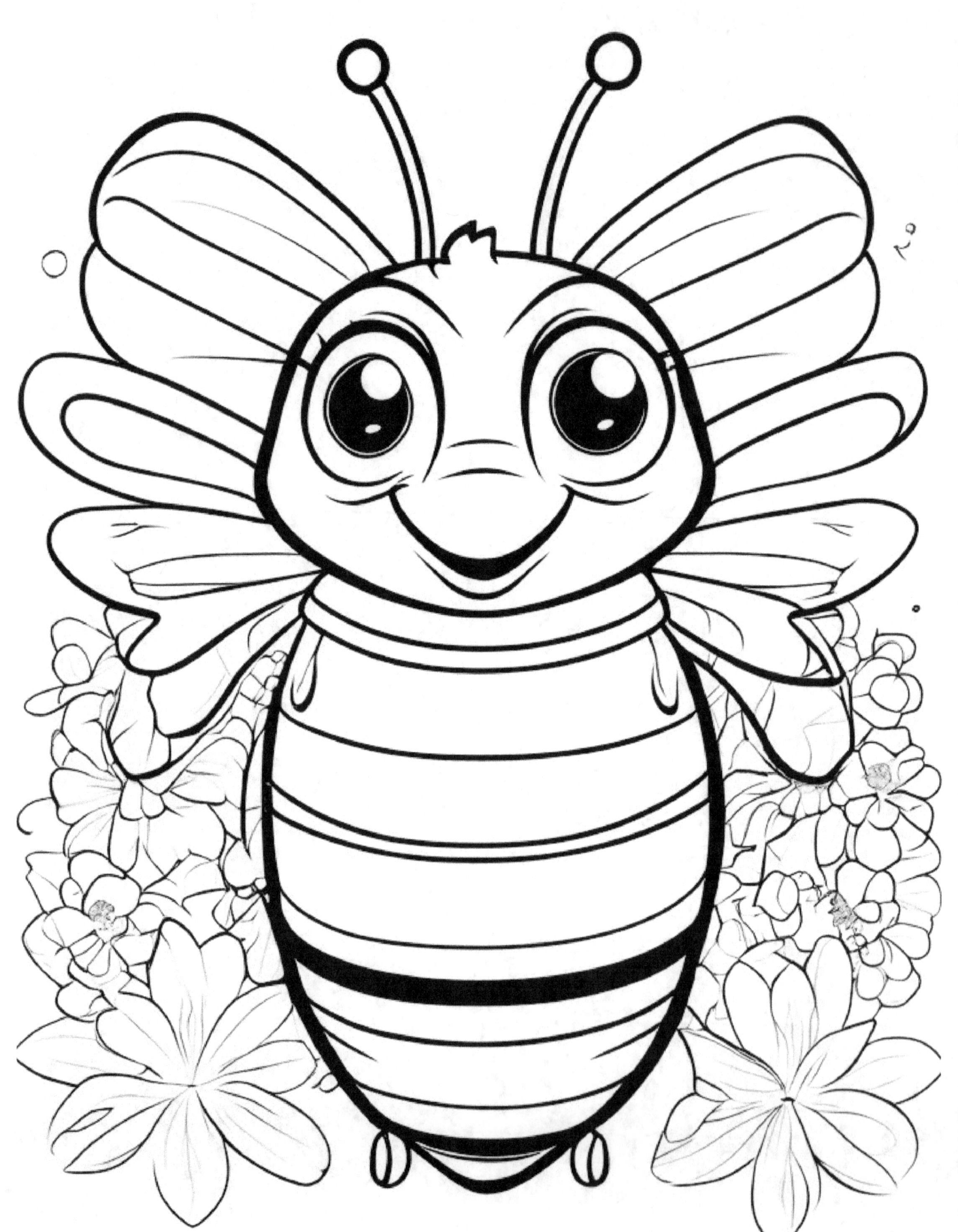